Terence Roberts was born in Ruthin, North Wales, before moving to Halifax, West Yorkshire, as a young child. It is here, on the Grove Estate in Ovenden, that he grew up from boy to man.

He qualified as a probation officer at the University of Huddersfield, then worked for the probation service in Merseyside and West Yorkshire. At the age of 50, he followed his dream and went to live in Ireland where he worked for the Irish Probation Service in Limerick.

Now retired, he lives in O'Brien's Bridge, County Clare, with his family of horses, donkeys and retired greyhounds. This period of his life in Ireland proved inspiration for the memoir, *All Because of Daisy*.

This is dedicated to those people who made life on the Grove Estate in the '60s and '70s an unforgettable experience that moulded me into the character I am now. For my mother, Olwen May Roberts, who taught me about the goodness in life, plus, determination and courage, I will always be grateful for that education. For Alf Praulins, who treated me as a brother then and now, who showed me maturity and wisdom many years before I could recognise them.

It is also dedicated to my old girlfriend, Jenny, who after all these years hasn't changed and still speaks to me. Likewise, to Ian Barker, my very good friend who grew up on the estate and discovered both the world and wisdom throughout his career. To those old Yorkshire friends and many others too, I value their continuing friendship after all these passing years.

It is also dedicated to the former staff and pupils of the Highlands Grammar School, not least Mr David Bannister.

Most importantly, it is dedicated to those who suffer and fight domestic violence.

Terence Roberts

RED BRICKS AND LOOSE DOGS

AUSTIN MACAULEY PUBLISHERS™

LONDON • CAMBRIDGE • NEW YORK • SHARJAH

A CIP catalogue record for this title is available from the British Library.

ISBN 9781035813216 (Paperback)
ISBN 9781035813223 (ePub e-book)

www.austinmacauley.com

First Published 2024
Austin Macauley Publishers Ltd®
1 Canada Square
Canary Wharf
London
E14 5AA

Thank you to Brian McNulty and Denis Bartley for your encouragement and support during this adventure. Likewise, the same must be said of my old friend, Alf Praulins, who also provided recollections that confirmed my very own perspective of those unforgettable people and events that made this journey possible.

Foreword

Looking for the truth.

'We are born innocent and only through life's experiences do we become corrupted. Somewhere along life's journey, it is to be hoped that we are able to recover some of that lost innocence before it is too late. Shame and guilt are like dirty white shirts and sinners came to me to do their washing. They should have done their own'.

So wrote Father Jim, weeks before he died. He had reached the end of his life, carrying the burden of others in the form of secrets and guilt. Secrets and guilt that others had expected the good Father to forgive in the name of God.

Other than his vows, Father Jim was as normal as any man, no doubt with weaknesses we could see and desires that we couldn't. He was a man of measured words and there was a wisdom about him that I always listened to.

I firmly believed that after searching through his own memories, he had come to realise that the way to salvation, peace and freedom was through each person washing their own 'dirty white shirts'.

As he approached his final weeks, it was as though he realised that he could not issue visas to heaven after all. In those measured words, I sensed that he discovered his own truths, not least that each of us was accountable to ourselves first and then to God.

When he passed away, I could hear those words with increasing frequency. I began to ask myself if my own life meant anything at all, had I been a decent person who did his best to give and not to take.

Here I was, on the lazy side of mid-life, retired on health grounds and beginning to search for myself again. Beginning to look in the mirror and see the lines on my face for the first time. Beginning to wonder where they came from, where I came from, where the innocence of birth went to and why.

So, as of today, I'm ignoring those wise owls who often yell 'don't look back', for whatever reason, because looking forward right now isn't the most inspiring view. I've decided to try and find the truth about my early years, that bedrock of my character and learning.

As Father Jim said, the only way to find the truth, to liberate oneself, was to search your own soul in the minefield of your past. For only you know your perspective on life's events and only you know the validity of your own conscience. That is the personal power that we all own.

I can only start to do this by going back in time, to my adopted homeland, in Yorkshire in the 1960s and '70s. In this journey, I hope to rediscover the people and places that I shared my ordinary life with, to recollect those events that stole away my innocence whilst hardening me for the wider world.

During my travels from boyhood to manhood, I needed to rediscover my truths, as I alone see them. Only then can I start to do my own dirty washing.

Chapter 1
Red Bricks and Loose Dogs

In the late 1960s and '70s, we used to say 'we live up the Grove'. It was a sprawling council estate, the size of the Russian Empire, covering most of Ovenden in the Yorkshire town of Halifax.

It spread, like it does now, way beyond Grove Avenue to adjoining estates of red brick houses, all seemingly built the same to house thousands of working-class families in the area. I recall that it was often described as the biggest council estate in Europe at the time, which it must have been if it was bigger than the Soviet Union.

On second thoughts, I'm not sure about that but as a scrawny nipper, it looked massively large and intimidating to me, as though this was the world itself. Of course, you could see green fields in the distance, up the hill towards Queensbury, but then, living on the estate was the only world I knew. It was a dull, harsh and uncompromising environment, a factory of houses to accommodate those with no other options.

In 1968, I was ten years old when we moved there, just myself, Taffy the dog and my parents. We lived at number 15, Grove Avenue, not far up from the police station. In fact, you'd think that being so close to a police station, maybe a hundred yards to the door, would give you a sense of security, of safety.

But no, the estate never gave that sense of security. But it was home and we made the most of it. It's vast size was intimidating for a young boy growing up. If you caught the right bus from Halifax town centre to the 'bottom of the Grove', there was no problem getting home safely.

But if you had to catch the bus to the 'top of the Grove', you simply jumped off at the bus stop and ran down the Grove as fast as you could. You didn't know too many young lads at the top, they had their friends while you had yours further down the Grove.

So, in fear of being challenged by those who lived and played at the top, it made sense to rapidly run down the hill, to avoid abuse or bullying and more importantly, to escape the array of loose dogs, who seemed to relish the chase of an invading nipper on their territory.

You couldn't go twenty yards without one or two dogs scenting your fear and setting off in full pursuit, chasing you so fast, like greyhounds after the hare, hoping that you'd hit the deck in your desperation to get home.

And when you hit the deck, there was inevitably broken glass and occasional stones to roll into. Yes, it was red bricks, loose dogs and broken glass all the way home.

Funnily enough, while those of us who lived at the bottom of the Grove kept close to home, you'd often see our own pet dogs go roaming north, up to the top of the estate and even beyond to Wheatley.

Taffy, our brown and black mongrel, would go walk about every day, enticing dozens of dogs when she came into season. She was a tough old bitch, fearless and independent and I know she was the first girl that I fell in love with, followed closely by Lily Webster.

My beloved Taffy, clearly had the same enticing charms as sweet Lily Webster, luring dogs of all shapes and sizes on to the estate. Many of the dogs came in pairs, which I never understood at the time but on reflection, it only seemed natural for dogs to go courting in twos and threes.

Just like we did a few years later as we went from pub to pub in Halifax town centre. But watching them court old Taffy was my first introduction to the term that made parents uncomfortable back then, 'sex education'.

We'd be in bed and they'd come howling, calling on Taffy as though she was royalty. I remember two particular regular suitors even now, one being an Alsatian type mongrel, followed by his mate, a short haired, scruffy looking terrier or something resembling a terrier.

I don't think there were too many pure bred dogs on the estate at that time and these two hounds certainly weren't that. They were mean-looking dogs, no doubt good 'ratters' and good scrappers and no doubt well loved by their owners.

But they were the odd couple as far as a pair of courting dogs seeking sweethearts were concerned.

I remember them well because of their persistence, culminating with Taffy being locked in lust with the bigger dog, their union being impossible to break until we used buckets of water, a broom handle and language you'd never hear in nearby St Malachy's church.

At one point, I thought they'd never separate. It was the first time that I'd seen a live sex show, in fact it was the only time. Then, a few months later, there was the result; Taffy doing all the work, safely delivering her six pups, which were all to be homed in due course.

There was no need for vets at that time, as dear old Taffy knew how to conceive and how to deliver, with no help other than bedding, water and love. She was the first dog that I ever had, ever learnt to love as a scruffy young boy and that loving relationship with dogs was born to last forever.

Looking back and considering how my life later revolved around greyhound racing, that boyhood love affair with my first ever dog, sweet and bold Taffy, was something I owed for much of my future happiness.

Those early days in the maze of red brick houses and loose dogs made me, though I never knew it at that time.

Chapter 2
Feisty Scottish Terriers, The McClairs

Across the road from our house lived Jimmy McClair and his parents, plus his older teenage sister, Agnes, who we all admired in our formative years. We'd hear her coming from miles away.

The clippity-clop of high heeled shoes that she just about managed to walk in. Then there was the smell of her perfume, gliding up the Grove as she walked uphill from the bus stop. As soon as you heard the clippity-clop, you'd wait for the whiff of perfume chasing not far behind. Then she'd appear, a tight blouse trying to contain her breasts or tits as we called them back then, as young boys dropped their jaws to see a real woman.

At that time, before we reached our teenage years, all we could do was gawp and wonder, then we'd run off to play football again without knowing that our time would come in a few years to fully understand why we were different from girls, as our parents always told us back then.

Mr and Mrs M, as we called them, originated from Glasgow and had landed in Yorkshire in search of work in the woollen mills in the late 1950s. It was hard to understand their

Scottish accents but we always understood their kindness, especially Mrs M, who often called the boys along to taste a rare treat that she brought from her homeland, shortbread biscuits.

As for Aggie, she didn't seem to do much baking herself, as she was too busy flirting with young men and even the older blokes. She was also one of those older girls who used to make me blush crimson by simply calling out, "hiya Terry."

In fact, none of the other younger boys knew what to say, not even a word, when an older girl spoke to us. But entering that magical world of puberty, we were well able to imagine what we wanted to say to her.

But we never did, because red cheeks and blustering words for innocent boys were something we tried to fend off every day.

Her brother Jimmy was built like a miner's whippet, who modelled himself on the legendary Jimmy Johnstone, the great Scottish winger who was as famous for his exploits on the pitch as off it.

So much so, that young Jimmy McClair was being watched at an early age by scouts from local professional clubs, including Huddersfield Town. But like most young talented footballers growing up in uncompromisingly tough environments, the temptations that the teenage years offered brought about his downfall, especially where drink was concerned.

No doubt he also followed his father's example. Yes, Mr M, like many of the men on the estate, would wander home drunk, swaying in the breeze just like Jimmy Johnstone drifting between two hardened Rangers' defenders towards the goal.

Though Mr McClair's goal was just to get home safely to his 'Wee Mary', often falling between the privets next to their crumbling wooden gate. Getting himself up, he'd stumble to the front door, serenading his beloved sweetheart in hope of comfort and warmth for the rest of the night.

Then in the following hour, you'd hear Mary give her husband hell, he responding with flailing arms and 'f' words by the second. Then as Jimmy's dad eventually fell onto the grubby carpet, as he usually did, Wee Mary riddled his pockets for pound notes and any lose change.

Like most of the women and children who lived with drunks on the estate, the only way to get the shop-keeping or money to pay the bills was to go through the pockets of their drunken husbands that night, otherwise it would only go to the landlord of the Noah's Ark the next day.

For young Jimmy, emptying his father's pockets when he was drunk was the only way that he ever had 'pocket money'. I guess that is where the term came from.

Yes, young Jimmy no doubt learnt that getting drunk was the norm. Like the rest of us, he began his affair with alcohol drinking Strongbow cider on the grass mound by the old folk's bungalow.

The local corner shop sold large flagons of cider, seemingly to each and every youngster who had enough to copper up for a bottle or two. And, of course, Jimmy McClair, the talented kid with twinkling feet that attracted the interest of local soccer scouts, fell by the wayside just as easily as his father fell through the privets in the garden.

When he was fifteen, he managed to get a trial with Huddersfield Town, on pure natural talent alone. But despite scoring in that trial and impressing in the junior teams, he was never offered a contract. Why? Simply because he made the wrong choices at a very young age and those who thought they knew better, considered him too much of a risk.

Even in those days, soccer clubs did their homework on young talent. They'd ask around, use their connections, to see what kind of lad a young player was off the field. On one occasion, as he turned sixteen, Jimmy celebrated his birthday with Dicky Freer, by sneaking into town, blagarding their way into a town centre pub for the first time.

Dicky Freer was much older but not wiser than Yorkshire's own, young Jimmy Johnstone. As Dicky went to the front of the bar in the Upper George, Jimmy celebrated his coming of age two years early, sipping pints of best bitter at the back of the bar room, away from the sight of the bar staff.

Only when he'd consumed too much and needed the toilet was he rumbled as he stumbled over the feet of other drinkers.

When Dicky and Jimmy were eventually kicked out of the Upper George, they decided enough was enough, making their way home on the last bus. But the last bus home when you're not used to a gutful of Yorkshire bitter on a cold night can be a painful journey, even if it's only twenty minutes or so.

As they got off the bus on Ovenden Road, their bladders were bursting for relief like they'd never known. In a drunken haze, Jimmy followed Dicky around the back of the nearest wall, out of sight of the cars passing on the Ovenden Road.

Unfortunately, while it was a wall protecting them from onlookers on the main road, it backed on to the inner yard of the police station. When their piss blew fumes of steam as they relieved themselves, laughing merrily as they did, they were brought down to earth by the sound of Sergeant Taylor.

"Now lads, you'd better come inside for a chat." And of course, they had to.

Jimmy didn't help himself when he replied to the Sergeant's leading question.

"And what's your name, son, and your address?"

To which, Jimmy replied, "Frank Worthington and I live in Leicester."

Well, even Sergeant Taylor could deduce that this wasn't Frank Worthington, the England international centre forward, so after giving Jimmy that old, cold, bobby's stare of bygone days, he brought young Jimmy down to earth.

"Your name, son, and your address and this time, you're not Billy Bremner by any chance?"

Within five minutes, Jimmy was being marched up the hill to number 12, Grove Avenue, almost blubbering like a baby. When Mary, his mother, appeared at the door, the Sergeant said:

"I'm bringing your son home safely, Mrs Worthington or is it Mrs Bremner?"

Given his age, old Sergeant Taylor cautioned Jimmy, with some ferocity, while Jimmy's mother could only say, "wait 'til your father gets home, just yee wait, son."

But that scare, that caution, never made the difference to Jimmy's life. As for Dicky Freer, he delighted in telling all and sundry about the night they were arrested and when Jimmy McClair wet his pants on the way home.

Jimmy never got over the embarrassment but worse still, he never learnt from the experience. In fact, he drank even more.

It's a story commonly heard in a thousand towns around the world; young, talented, local heroes falling at the earliest fences, often simply because of a lack of parental guidance and discipline.

Instead, Jimmy went on to live what was sometimes cruelly considered, 'a no man's life', governed by his drinking and inability to hold down a job. Years later, I heard that he had a spell in prison, again linked to his drinking and lack of self-discipline.

Jimmy wasn't a bad lad by any means and he had far more talent than the rest of us who wanted to be professional footballers. But when his chances came and passed, he could never learn from the rejection; going from incarceration to death in his thirties through liver failure.

Chapter 3
The Vardys

Up the road from the McClair's lived the Vardys, perhaps the best looking family for miles around. Surely, their inherent good looks would bring them happiness? Unfortunately, despite their striking features, running through the family from top to bottom, it seemed that even they had difficult times in pursuit of happiness.

George, the father, resembled a better looking Sean Connery but was riddled with laziness and an inability to say a sentence without using the 'f' word and worse still, the 'c' word.

Every sentence, however innocent in intention, had an expletive in it, so George was never going to get a job in the diplomatic core or even as a porter in the George Hotel.

"Them fucking dafs are fucking beautiful, Vi', fucking beautiful, if I say so myself," he'd shout to his pretty wife, Violet.

As George proved, good looks weren't everything, not only because of his love of foul language but also because of his careless hands. He just couldn't control them, he simply didn't have a moral conscience.

I remember when I was twelve years old, waiting to buy my dad's two bottles of Webster's bitter from Dutney's, which he had every Thursday for breakfast, when George walked in.

As Mr Dutney turned his back, George picked up two packets of Woodbines, then leaned into my ear to whisper, "you saw nothing or you're fucking dead, son."

Then, when Mr Dutney turned around, oblivious to the crime, George said, "sorry Charlie, I've totally forgot what I fuckin came in for, it'll come back to me, see you later."

And of course, I said nothing. Because I'd learnt at an early age that if someone on the Grove said they'd batter you, they weren't going to just dip you gently into fish batter for Friday tea time.

Yes, looking back I can see why Gorgeous George, as he was known, never made it in life; not least because he inevitably did his share of time in prison. Though to be fair to him, he did try to set up his own business to supplement his dole and family allowance payments.

Being a keen racing fan who, like my father and others, considered local bookies and pubs as their offices, he inevitably went into the racing industry, albeit very briefly. His greatest moment in life was watching the Race of the Century, involving his beloved Grundy and Bustino.

He loved horseracing and he reckoned that when he was in the bookies or the pub, he was doing business rent-free and didn't have to pay overheads like heating bills. Or business rates.

Or tax, other than betting tax. So, he came up with the idea of selling racing tips to mug punters around the country from a tax-free haven.

This all transpired when his son, Barry, was asked to do some labouring to bolster up his dole money, a couple of miles from the estate on the road to Mixenden.

After flattening the garage at the rear, Barry learnt that the owner, who'd inherited the property from his recently bereaved mother, would be returning to Yorkshire in six weeks' time to totally redecorate it.

Before then, Barry and his mate Pin Head were to clear the house and prepare the walls for decorating. Easy money, thought Barry. Anyway, once Barry's father George heard that the house was to be empty for the next six weeks, he decided to set up a short term tipping service.

He managed to place adverts in one sporting paper claiming, 'Whitehorse Winners are a sure thing', posing as a horse racing gallops expert in the north. It was a scam, used all over the country to catch out mug punters.

They would receive two hot tips for the coming Saturday's big races in return for the reasonable sum of a pound a go. In the next few weeks, despite sending out losing tips for most of the races, Barry and his father made a fair few quid from hopeful gamblers, using an address that couldn't be traced to them when the house owner moved in a few weeks later.

Though, when the new owner started to get offensive mail in the form of angry complaints from punters having been sent out useless tips, the matter inevitably landed down at the local police station.

The scam only lasted a few short weeks and was never repeated but using an address that had no ties to the Vardys, proved that they weren't only a good looking family but shrewd enough too, in a limited way.

In fact, while young Barry mistakenly thought he was the shrewdest, his older sister, Suzy, was no fool either. She was a very pretty teenager who realised that she was no academic, nor was she a hard worker.

Suzy was at least sharp enough to know her own limitations, which is a life-skill in itself. So, having been told she was a pretty little thing all her teenage years, she decided that her looks were her only way to a better future.

Suzy, as far as I can remember, never courted boys from the estate. She believed they were all like her father and brothers; that is men who'd achieve little in life other than an annual holiday to Whitby and who'd be reporting to a Probation Officer for as long as they'd be signing on at the dole office in town.

For Suzy, blessed with her mother's stunning looks and enticing figure, boys from the estate were losers who would never give her the life she craved for.

She loved watching *The Main Chance* on TV, a drama series about a northern solicitor, as good looking as her father but who had pots of legitimate gold, plus the heady lifestyle becoming of his respected business.

So, with this realisation in mind, the only men she had time for were men with soft hands, fast cars and bursting wallets. In the end, she managed to escape her natural environment of the Grove, eventually catching a solicitor from Ripponden after falling pregnant within months of the courtship.

Inevitably, the relationship floundered when her lawyer boyfriend realised his predicament. But Suzy had already secured a comfortable future for herself and her forthcoming child through a large, grubby financial settlement that he was more than happy to pay.

As soon as he realised that he had been trapped into fatherhood by a girl from the other side of the tracks, her boyfriend paid her out of his life far quicker than she came into it.

No doubt he did his homework on the Vardy family when the pregnancy led to discussion about marriage. I reckon the prospect of George Vardy 'f'ing and blinding during the wedding speeches and at the child's christening, caused him much anxiety.

I also suppose, that he contemplated whether the child should be put on the list for Woodhouse Grove School or Ovenden Secondary Modern. Either way, as the two parents went their separate ways, it was as usual, the child who suffered without a stable family background.

However, I heard some years ago that Suzy never returned to the Grove to live, nor to even visit her family. She'd escaped to what she thought was a better world, happy to turn her back on both her own family and the embarrassed sire of her only child.

In the end, she wanted for nothing financially but she had sold her soul along the way. Watching *The Main Chance* had paid comfortable dividends, but at what cost to her reputation and her son's future?

Chapter 4
Handsome Is as Handsome Does

As for Suzy's brother, Barry, he also used his good looks to his advantage but never to secure a sound financial future as his sister had done.

He was destined to go no further than his father, in terms of social mobility, simply because he was as lazy as his dad and he had inherited his dad's genetic gift of using the 'f' and 'c' words as though they were magnets to fine social intercourse.

Like his father, Barry enjoyed prison food and knew his way to the probation office blindfold from his mid-teenage years and I am told, to well into his fifties.

No, Barry's harnessing of his inherited good looks paid dividends in other, more basic, walks of life. When he was fourteen, while the rest of his peers fantasised about scoring at Wembley or Elland Road, good looking Barry decided to score elsewhere.

Fifty yards or so from his front door lived Jeanette Ackroyd and her husband, Frank. He was a mystery, in his mid-thirties, never socialising with neighbours and almost too shy to say 'hello' when you crossed him in the street.

He worked in the North Sea, on the oil rigs and his time back home was very much spent exclusively with his attractive wife. No one knew much about Jeanette either and the only time she was seen outside was when she was going to and fro' with shopping.

She didn't work, nor was she ever seen leaning over the garden fence, talking to Mrs Gallagher on one side or the Daley's on the other. Yet, Barry Vardy, teenage Barry who should have been kicking a ball around with his mates on the green, did know her and knew her far too well for a lad of fourteen.

One night, when we were camping out on the green, we lay in the tent, torches alight, the three of us. Alf, Barry and myself. As we quietly giggled about the girls in the O'Neill family that had just moved in to number 45, we heard footsteps in the grass and sensed we had company.

It was Lily Webster, brazen as ever, fishing to join the three of us in the tent, to flaunt her wares and saucy teasing, knowing full well that she'd have some of us blushing through our innocence.

Yes, Lily was a temptress to us all and she knew it. On that enlightening evening, she leaned into the tent, smelling of cheap sherry and her mother's lipstick, staring intently at young Master Vardy, then shaking her head with a knowing smile across her pretty face.

"Barry," she said, "have you been doing odd jobs again for Scrubber Ackroyd?"

Well, this was like a 'red rag to a bull' for young Barry, who lashed out with his boot to force Lily out of the tent, cursing and threatening as only he and his father could, the 'f' word bouncing off the 'c' word, time and time again.

Lily had touched the rawest nerve, though she probably assumed that Alf and I already knew the full story. But we knew nothing and as Barry left rapidly in embarrassment, both Alf and I began to ponder what had been going on behind closed curtains in the Ackroyd residency.

The next day Barry resurfaced, his blushes tempered with time and time enough for him to think of what to tell us, as he knew he'd be interrogated. Of the three of us, he was the handsome one, known locally as 'young Gregory Peck' and his good looks had found him opportunities that the rest of us could barely dream of.

It seemed that young Gregory Peck had met Mrs Ackroyd one afternoon as she struggled to carry her shopping bags up the hill. Naturally, she dropped a bag of the shopping then looked over to Barry to ask for his help.

Then, as one thing led to another and while her husband worked away on the oil rig, Barry found himself lured into her kitchen to place the bag of shopping onto the table. That was three weeks ago, Barry said.

Since then, every evening he'd been calling round to her house for his supper, sneaking round to the back door in the increasing darkness. When he was pushed to explain what she gave him for supper, he was desperate to keep his new found treasure private.

But he was unable to do so once Lily Webster saw him leave there one evening, red in the face under the glowing street lamps. Barry's confession to Alf and myself made us envious, as he'd used his film star good looks to break the ice and be the first of us to turn fantasy into reality.

That night, as we slept in the tent, we realised that Barry had crossed the line, easily seduced by a woman nearly twenty years older than himself. He'd been abused by her but he never saw it that way, even when she introduced him to her favourite sex toy.

She apparently called it her 'best friend' and proceeded to show young Barry why. That seedy, undoubtedly abusive and illegal affair seemed to lead him into a lifelong fetish for women much older than himself.

Even now, in his early sixties, he apparently lives with his partner of eighty having never lived with a woman of his own age. For myself and Alf, it was a wake-up call, a sign to realise that chasing that football around the green was a game that we'd have to move on from sooner or later. It was also a sign; never to carry shopping for Mrs Ackroyd.

However, a few weeks later, we saw Mr Ackroyd walk up the Grove, his bag over his broad shoulders, no doubt coming home from the oil rigs for his home comforts, to be welcomed by his lonely, forgotten wife.

Barry later told us that when he saw her husband walk up the street, built like a tank and firm of foot, he realised that he'd been where he shouldn't have been. While he would never forget his first joyful romps with a 'real woman', he admitted that he was too scared to continue bedding Mrs Ackroyd beyond those initial sexual skirmishes.

But it wasn't the fear of being battered by her husband that worried Barry. It was the fear of further public humiliation. The fact came to light, through our lovely Lily Webster, that Barry wasn't the first teenager that had been abused by Mrs Ackroyd and even Barry could guess that he wouldn't be the last.

Apparently, Mr Dutney's young lad, Norman, had spilled the beans to mischievous Lily that he'd also been introduced to Mrs Ackroyd's 'best friend', no doubt after helping her with her shopping!

Years down the line, we could look back and see that she was a sex offender, an efficient and dangerous one at that. She was no different than a man abusing underage males or females.

However, in one important subject, young Barry Vardy learnt more from Jeanette Ackroyd than from any book or lesson at school. He certainly learnt a different definition for the term 'best friend'.

How that grubby loss of innocence affected him in the years to come, only Barry would know and how many other young boys had their innocence stolen by Mrs Ackroyd, only she would know.

Chapter 5
Let Justice Be Done, The Smiths

Learning right from wrong often starts in the family home for most of us and then that learning is tested in the local community and beyond. Such was life on the Grove estate. And while Jeanette Ackroyd clearly got away with murder after abusing local youngsters, others paid the full price for similar misdemeanours. Ask Roy Smith.

The Smith family came from nowhere and it seemed that they went back there, all in the space of a couple of years. They were a mystery family living up the Grove. Like most families on the estate, they had little; certainly, no car, nor employment or any other trappings of reasonable comfort.

And they were even more secretive than the Ackroyd's, which looking back, might explain a few things. Susan was the youngest, fourteen years old when she arrived and only sixteen when she disappeared back into the wilderness.

All the young, local teenage girls tried to get her to join in with them but it was soon obvious that her parents, Roy and Bridget, didn't approve. From playing on the streets, under the evening lamplights, she seemed to vanish within a few months of arriving.

Quite naturally, the rumours began to spread when she skipped off school with increasing regularity. Then one day, some months later, the rumours ran riot when she was seen leaving the doctors with her mother, seemingly carrying more under her coat than a thick jumper.

Then just as quickly, she was a mother herself, without any sign of a father to the child, other than sinister rumours that Susan's own dad was responsible. I cannot recall what made people think that this was the case, nor was there any evidence of it in the subsequent years.

No firm evidence that is. But I remember as clear as day, that during Susan's pregnancy, her father, Roy reportedly took one hell of a beating near the wall adjacent to the run-down local factory.

After that he disappeared, never to be seen in the area again. Nobody held their hands up for the assault, for obvious reasons but rumours abounded about 'the five good men' and who they were.

The next year, both Susan and her mother, together with the young baby, disappeared back to 'nowhere' or somewhere, while the local community were left to ponder what exactly happened in that family and why Roy disappeared in a puff of smoke during her pregnancy.

Theories came to light about that fatal night when Roy Smith appeared to be the victim of street justice, meted out by local men, 'the five good men' who didn't trust the police to protect their children from sex offenders.

In fact, it was in those early years that I learnt that the law, the truth and justice itself, could be dirty bed-mates in life.

As a retired Probation Officer, I always worked within the law but I'm now speaking about the reality of life on the estate at that time. I learnt from the estate that people didn't always live within the law, though most tried to and it was easy to see that justice came in many shapes and forms.

So, when Roy Smith disappeared after that night, among rumours that he'd made his own daughter pregnant while also 'sniffing around' other teenagers on the estate, you can only put two and two together.

Local legends abound in every community and the story unfolded that Roy was beaten up, his tail chopped off and then fed to pigs in Stainland. Whether that is or isn't justice, you will have to make your own mind up.

However, the story itself was a message to every other abuser; that the hungry pigs in Stainland would always need feeding.

Chapter 6
Blessings and Nightmares

In the '60s and '70s, there was no evidence whatsoever, of illegal drug use in the Grove estate. But many families had arrived there with some history of alcohol misuse. Most nights it was likely that one father or another would wander up the Grove, drunk as a skunk, as they say, often singing or occasionally ranting away to their hearts content.

When Mr McClair blurted out, "you take the high road and I'll take the low road," you could be sure that his wife and son Jimmy were dreading him falling through the door. Likewise Alf's father, who I'd see walking past the window talking aloud in his native Latvian tongue after a night in the Ovenden Cross. At which point, I'd know that Alf would soon be going through the same experiences that every child of an alcoholic goes through when a drunken parent staggers home. Hiding under the bed if you were small enough and getting ready to face violence if you were bigger.

Yet when we played in the streets in the coming days, the embarrassment of our fathers' drunken behaviour only lasted very briefly. Because while we were all embarrassed and were ashamed of our fathers, we also shared similar experiences.

Growing up witnessing and suffering domestic violence as a child was as normal as fish and chips at Friday tea time and watching Coronation Street. For many of us, it was simply our way of life.

Occasionally, one of us would turn up to play football the next day with a mark on our face or body and, sometimes, you wouldn't see one of us for a couple of days for the same reason. But there never seemed to be a social worker or anyone else who really cared about mothers and children living in violence.

Yes and when the singing stopped and the drunken father was behind the front door that was never the end of it. It was only the beginning. On those nights, my mother and I would have been trying to enjoy Coronation Street or some game show or maybe a televised soccer match.

But our nerves would be dancing on egg shells, knowing full well that 'the old man' would be coming home drunk later that night.

We loved each other's company, Mum and I, and it was us against the world in terms of how we had to deal with a drunken, violent man, who had no regard or real love for us. If he did love in any way, why did he keep on repeating the intimidation and violence?

Brother Ronnie was away, serving his country for most of the time in the '60s and early '70s and the rest of our family were mainly in North Wales, oblivious to our life in Yorkshire. So Mum and I went through that hell alone, learning to survive a life dominated by a bully.

We were on the front line, just like millions have been over the years and to this very day. There were some nights that he'd come home so legless that it was an absolute blessing, because he couldn't even throw a punch or grab Mum's hair.

Yes, he had that awful habit of pulling her by the hair, ranting and raving, like she was a toy doll worth nothing to him or herself for that matter. An object, just an object.

He was nasty with his words too, venomous at times, more poisonous than a snake. "Tell the bastard who his father is," sticks with me forever.

"Why can't you keep the house clean, you dirty bitch?" was a regular taunt at a woman who worked every day in the Gas Board to pay every bill and who did keep the house clean as well.

Then, after more abuse to the both of us, if he was paralytic he'd fall down before going into a drunken sleep. At which point, we thanked God, then emptied his pockets to take some cash towards our food and bills.

Then, we'd caringly take him upstairs to bed, before returning to our evening in front of the TV. That would be considered a quiet night. Later that evening, Mum would go to bed praying he was still asleep with drink, on many occasions having to then sleep in a chair rather than lie on a warm, wet mattress.

But when he was drunk but not incapable, when he was alert enough to be viscous for a couple of hours, it was a nightmare.

It would be a nightmare because we always knew what he was capable of. A pattern developed, when he'd return home in a bitter mood, having spent all his money that night, having no more money for booze in the coming days.

On those occasions, you knew he'd make life on his return home so miserable that it would break my mother down again, dreading the next day when he'd take the onslaught down to the Gas Board where she worked.

There, he'd shame her into giving him more money to get drunk again. It was a cycle of abuse that he controlled. He knew that he only had to turn up and wait outside her office and she'd break.

On other occasions, he'd get on the bus in town after she had embarked at the previous stop, only to talk loudly and drunkenly to her in front of everyone. He knew that shaming her in public would hurt and manipulate her and for whatever reason, there was never anybody brave enough to stop him.

That only stopped when I became big enough to take him on, at least to stand up and call him 'an old bastard' amidst other insults. Looking back, I did myself no favours through such language or behaviour but I felt I had no choice other than to abuse him like he abused others.

His actions brought out the worst in me. My father was the man who introduced me to the meaning of 'hate'. Nowadays, I still don't know if I hated him or if I just hated the things he did.

Hate is a powerful emotion, one of the most destructive and my father brought hatred into my life like no one else has ever done.

One thing he had taught me was that you had to stand up to a bully, even if it costs you a belt or two. And my father was the biggest bully. Seeing my mother survive over the years taught me empathy and a total disregard for men who abused others as though it was their divine right.

At least I witnessed a man that I'd never want to be. I thank God for that education in life. Like many bullies, he was seemingly popular among his friends or cronies as I called them, as he bought his round in the Railway or the Noah's Ark.

They'd share the craic for hours, as though they were naturally entitled to drink and gamble the housekeeping money away, knowing that their women were at home ready to pick up the pieces, to feed them, nurse them, show love of all sorts out of either duty or fear.

I remember the nights when he would go to bed drunk, leaving mum and I downstairs to watch the TV. Then the times when he would wake up and start banging on the bedroom floor, before shouting down, "come to bed, Olwen."

He'd repeat this and mum would ignore it until he came to the top of the stairs and shout again, "come to bed, Olwen." The same old words, the same old order from a drunk who still thought he was a Sergeant Major.

Then, in time, my mother would know that she had no choice and would go to his bed. I can only imagine, with disgust, what may have happened when she went upstairs at his command. Because it was always at his command.

And yet while those days of predictable drunken violence were shared by many of the teenagers on the estate, each family experienced their own particular difficulties. It was always the father, the man, who had the money to entertain himself while they went without.

It was the man who had the freedom to socialise and behave as he wanted, while the woman's place was back in the house. Not just doing all the domestic jobs but rearing the children, stitching patches onto trousers, smoking nervously in wait of the threats and violence and simply knowing that life outside the family 'home' was not allowed.

Nor did visitors come inside, certainly not to pop in and see how you were. For the home of a domestic abuser is a place where a family barely exists and hardly anyone visits.

The loneliness of a victim is like solitary confinement in a prison but with no protection at all.

This is why my mother and I stood together and even when there was no physical violence, there was the threat of shame and belittlement.

Yes, I recall some distastefully embarrassing occasions in the family home, which explained why it was a no-go zone for visitors. One particularly distasteful experience occurred when I was about twelve years of age, having joined the Halifax Subbuteo League, a league for children obsessed with the carpet football game that was so popular fifty odd years back.

I remember that when I joined the league, my father was away on one of his road trips. He would disappear once every year or so, claiming that he needed to 'live rough', to try and destroy himself by drinking with homeless men and women around the country.

It never made sense but we enjoyed it when he went and we didn't even care how he survived away from home. The feeling was mutual, I'm sure. He'd pack his bag and walk off one day, maybe going fruit picking in Worcestershire, just anything to get away.

Or maybe he had another woman elsewhere in the country? We didn't care, we just enjoyed the peace of his absence, a time when we would laugh and never worry what the evening would bring. In fact, I always wished he'd never come back and while Mum never said it, I'm sure she felt the same.

On this particular occasion, having joined the Subbuteo league, my first game was an away fixture in one of the 'posher' areas of Halifax, Heckmondwyke. Arriving by bus, I knocked on the door of this detached house with a beautiful garden.

Inside, I saw that the Subbuteo pitch was laid out on a very large table in a big room, where my opponent's mother welcomed me with smiles and refreshments. I felt a little overawed with the plush surroundings and the welcome from 'nice people', especially when his father joined us to watch the game unfold.

His dad was kind, he talked to me as though I mattered, asked me about school and sports that I played. He reminded me of my Uncles in Wales and he was so different from my father.

Yes, there was a warmth there but I'll never forget feeling somewhat overawed by the setting whilst appreciating the politeness that made me feel happy for that afternoon. Was this normality?

If only I lived nearer, this would have been a nice family, living in a different world that I would like as friends. But that was always going to be impossible because I came from the wrong side of the tracks.

That fact was reinforced the following weekend when I had to return the compliment by hosting the home game against the same boy. I only agreed to this because Dad was still away 'finding' himself in ale, cider and whisky or even worse, with his friends around the country.

And as for Mum, she was her wonderful self, making our humble home warm and welcoming, with orange Club biscuits and sweet fizzy pop. However, we never had the luxury of a large table, not even a large room, so I laid out the green carpet pitch on the floor.

The settee to one touchline, facing the fire and the two single chairs behind each goal. Then we kicked off and played as young boys do, very much as they do when they are impassioned by soccer.

I can't remember how the game was going but it was an afternoon where, despite knowing that my home was nothing compared to his, I felt comfortable, enjoying the company within those walls.

Then half time came, with Mum offering something or other to two growing lads. Then, like a thief in the dark of an alley way, he arrived; yes, he arrived from his wanderings, drunk as a skunk.

I will never forget it until the day I die. When he arrived, I think I learnt what blushing really meant as Mum tried to usher him into the kitchen, amid a few words and drunken giggles from my father.

"No," he insisted, he wanted to watch the boys play their game, eventually insisting that he did from the comfort of his own armchair. As this unfolded, I tried to spare my blushes by focusing on the game, encouraging my new found opponent and friend to do the same.

Then as time passed, I could hear the old man snore as he always did, only to wake up in haste a few minutes later as a plate of his teeth dropped out of his gaping jaws, saliva running down his chin.

Then back to sleep and for a while, as I pushed my players around the green carpet of a pitch, I sensed the worst was over as we approached the final whistle. Win, lose or draw was never an issue, it didn't matter anymore.

My embarrassment was complete, regardless of the outcome. But I soon learnt then, never to think that the worst was over when the worst had never even begun. It was a lesson for life that I learnt that day, one which made me cautious in my future years, never to take anything for granted.

That lesson, that lifelong lesson, began as we approached full time, when I noticed trickling fluid coming from my father's brown pants, as he had one leg either side of the goal posts, slumped in drunken dreams in his comfortable chair.

And as I saw him wet himself in his slumber, my heart crumpled; from which I've never recovered, even after all these years. All I can remember is making apology after apology, my mother doing the same, adding that my father had a medical problem that he couldn't control.

My poor friend left, the points from the match inevitably in the bag but, no doubt, forever badly traumatised from the experience.

That was my second game in the Halifax Subbuteo League and my last. I remember the tears and rightful rage of my mother as she screamed at my father for his disgusting behaviour that shamed us all.

Then when we told him what he'd done in his drunken state, he merely laughed. I have learnt that life flows like a river of pride and shame and that afternoon, it flowed of shame down my father's pants.

While it hurt then and still angers me now, I am certain that it hurt my mother even more. As for the young lad who witnessed it all, I cringe when I think that he would have gone home to his loving family to tell the tale of how the other half lives.

I just hope he's put the memory of that day out of his head because I haven't to this day.

Chapter 7
Broken Men and Heroic Women

Looking back, the 'normality' of violent drunken men on the estate takes some explaining. No doubt, there was a culture of hard drinking in the community as there was in many other communities. No doubt there were many families that never suffered from drink related domestic violence. But there were too many families who did.

Maybe it was that alcohol abuse was often a way to cope, to forget the reality of a hard life. And maybe the war was a factor, with 'victorious heroes' returning home to unemployment or relative poverty when they were already broken through their experiences of war.

Broken men returning home. Their women often scarred by their own losses through war, for they lost much too. Mr McClair, my father, Taffy Roberts, Alf's father and others, all wore different coloured uniforms when they marched off to war as wide-eyed young men but they all lost something during those six years of hell.

If they didn't lose their life or a limb, they lost their innocence. Many also lost their drive and hope, especially those returning to the dole queue or dead-end jobs that every day reminded them that their future was limited.

And for many, of all classes and backgrounds, while the shrapnel and bullets had ceased and they could sleep with their loved ones again, they never slept well. The sounds, the sights, the anxiety before the next dawn in modern warfare, never left many men who were lucky enough to return.

Returning often in guilt, while their buddies died, in bits and pieces, bone and flesh, resting memories in the survivor's eyes and souls, which would never go away. Or maybe returning in guilt after killing an enemy soldier for reasons that were often forgotten both then and now, other than the reason to kill a man before he kills you. No wonder there were so many broken men returning home, despite having being told they had won the war.

Those countless broken men, most who barely uttered a word about their experiences overseas. One day, I asked my father why he had no teeth at such a young age. He said that it was down to a German soldier's rifle butt-end catching him full in the mouth.

Imagining the pain of that, I then asked what became of the enemy soldier who did it. He said nothing. He just looked at me without any expression other than his bright blue eyes perhaps whispering, "well, that's the most ridiculous question I've ever heard."

I didn't pursue the matter, nor ask him about his other experiences. It was dead-man's land to go there, I thought. Looking back, I only wish I had asked more questions.

Yet and as much as these men came home, they left much of themselves in foreign parts, in Burma, North Africa, on French beaches and in cold Atlantic waters. And everywhere else, their souls sunk like their ships and their hearts.

Yes, they came home to wonderful women who served the country in ammunition factories, in the fields and often in uniformed service themselves, like my mother did in North Africa and the Mediterranean.

Yes, women who had kept the home fires burning when their men were away, who tried to keep normality as best they could, doing without love themselves, whilst scrimping and saving to bring up families, never knowing how or when it would end.

Then to pick up the pieces when their men returned, to try and make home loving and safe, whilst being reminded of their brokenness while sleeping with men who were never the same men after the bullets and bombs.

Often, it was strangers returning home to each other, man and wife, with their children there to witness it all in the future years. Broken people in broken families; there were too many of them who were young hopefuls before the war, who turned out to be middle-aged hopeless in the '50s, '60s and beyond.

No wonder drink and violence and the horrors of mental illness were so prevalent in that generation after the war, the so called 'Golden Generation'. November speeches in cenotaphs around the United Kingdom never talk of this when they remember the dead, injured and horrors of war.

The true glory of war must also include the return to life in peacetime, when families just got on with it, when they just tried to survive loss after loss.

In time, our parents then survived post war austerity, rationing and then slum clearance projects as the world slowly recovered from those six years of conflict. The NHS was born and the country began to find its feet again.

Then in the '60s, we were brought forward to a new world that would change attitudes to most forms of life forever. When we were told 'you've never had it so good', politicians weren't talking about the sexual liberation movement, though I suppose they could have meant that as well as employment and living standards.

Yes, it was a time of change, materially at least for the better or so we were told by politicians of the time. Life for our parents was as normal as it could have been, given the experiences of the past twenty five years or so.

But for children on the estate, I suppose it was playtime as usual. My generation simply grew up without the fears and constraints of our parent's generation and looking back, as children we were as free as birds.

Entertainment in the house evolved around a few TV channels, for many years in black and white. It opened our eyes to the world. We laughed at impersonators mimicking politicians, we enjoyed watching live sport, not least the 1966 World Cup final and we had our weekly fix of game shows and the soaps.

We saw how the other half lived. Then we'd go outside and play with boys and occasionally with girls, some of whom we remembered into our old age. As our parents tried to find their way in this modern world, so did we. But those days of childhood innocence were soon to disappear.

Chapter 8
Awakenings

Jonny Vardy was a child about four years younger than myself when I was at the age of increasing awareness. In most regards, he was like the rest us, being skinny and scruffy. But he was different because he was overly inquisitive, always sticking his nose in, as though nobody told him it was bad manners to do so.

One day, we were playing soccer in our usual spot, a couple of jumpers for posts, impersonating either Liverpool or Leeds heroes, playing make believe matches of a game called attack and defence.

This would go on all day, apart from when we had a break to swig 'Corporation pop', from the same glass bottle, filled with tap water. They were simple, uncomplicated times.

However, this day, as we older boys kicked and headed the ball until we dropped, young Jonny ran onto the pitch shouting, "Dad's shagging Mum, Dad's shagging Mum."

"How do you know, Jonny lad?" enquired his older brother, Barry.

"Because Mum's going 'ah, ah, ah, AH' and Dad's going 'come on Vi, come on Vi, come on Vi'. I've been watching them and it's still going on!"

Needless to say, we laughed for a moment at Jonny's rendition and the thought of him peering through a door when every other child was out and about playing into the evening. Then we just carried on with our game because that's what really mattered.

Yes, Jonny was a child growing up too fast. Another day, when the tent was still up by the side of the old folks' bungalow, we were running around the oval green as part of our unofficial Grove Olympics.

There were only six of us at the most; Alf, myself, Glen Butler, Nobby and a couple more. We all competed in sprint races, the long jump, even a high jump, though we often didn't manage to clear the old boxes, which acted as the high jump bar.

This time, it was the 5,000 metres final or something around that distance, probably twenty laps of the green. As we all went round, lap by lap, young Jonny could be seen wandering around the tent, having been told he was too young to challenge the big boys for the Olympic medals.

On approaching the tent, he then peered into the opening. As quiet as a mouse and Jonny wasn't much bigger than a mouse, he stuck his nose into the tent, then leaned forward in total silence to get an eyeful of what was occurring inside.

Then, after watching long enough to make an opinion, after seeing Wilfred Harden lying on his back, he burst into life like an Olympic sprinter, running straight on to our concrete athletics track to stop the race.

"Fuck off, Jonny, get off the track," one of us screamed.

"It's Harden," said Jonny, "he's pulling his cock, he's pulling his cock in the tent."

"How do you know, Jonny?" asked Alf with a smile.

"He's rubbing it up and down with a sock on it, just like our Barry does," was the reply.

Well, that was it. Cancelling the race, we all ran over to the tent, cursing Wilfred Harden, a much older lad, maybe eighteen or nineteen, shouting, "Willie's got a hard on, Willie Willie Harden, Willie's got a hard on."

Between us, we cursed him and shamed him for coming into our tent to play with himself. As for Jonny, God knows how he ever got over that sight but it never stopped him sticking his nose in where it was not wanted.

As for his older brother, Barry, you can be sure that he gave young Jonny a thick ear for telling the rest of us about his own self pleasuring with sweaty socks!

Then there was Bob Hardy, another of our mates who just couldn't avoid trouble. Living up the Grove was tough enough for every kid, boy or girl, because none of us ever went to diplomatic school.

We were told to play nicely but at the same time and perhaps more robustly, we were told never to back down from a fight. Of course we all played along, maybe soccer or 'find Hitler' or hide and seek, maybe cricket or another game born from our imagination.

Most of the time, it went well but if there was an occasional fall out, you'd rarely see a Dr Kissinger trying to keep the peace. I don't recall any of those childhood friends as being naturally vicious but when arguments flared, none of us had the skill to back down without losing face. And losing face on the estate was never an option.

As for my father, he would have battered me for dinner if I didn't prove I was a man but the fact is, like most boys, girls and people in general, I never enjoyed getting into a fight.

I've always believed that there is no pleasure in hurting anyone or anything. But certain situations in life make it a requirement to stand up for yourself. Especially when lessons of diplomacy to avoid a fight or a war were never passed on to us.

On this occasion, for whatever reason, Bob Hardy was cute enough for an eleven-year-old to start a fight between two boys, who later became friends for life.

That day, Bob was the umpire as we played a cricket match against the boys and girls from Athol Gardens, an adjacent street on the estate where our family would move to in later years.

Bob was quite good as an umpire, especially considering he had milk bottle bottom glasses and was as blind as a bat. But in time, as each player tried to make a mark on the game, we became frustrated with some of his misplaced decisions.

For some reason, he said it was against the rules to bowl bouncers. And for every bouncer I bowled, he gave a wide, an extra run to the opposition. Then, sensing the injustice and feeling that he was picking on me, little arguments became war.

Pretty soon things got out of hand and the 'gentleman's game', as it was described in those days, became far from gentlemanly.

But I can't remember how Alf became involved. He was the most sensible lad that I knew and definitely one of the most easy going. But from nowhere, we were stood facing each other, Alf with both his fists up, ready to protect himself in classical boxing style.

As for myself, I recall a few words being exchanged and while Alf then concentrated on the task ahead, to knock my block off, I swung punches that parted the air and probably knocked a few flies out.

But I could never lay a glove on Alf, despite my aggressive approach, as he picked me off like Mohammed Ali in a sparring session. I just couldn't work it out. He picked me off with punches to the head, a head that never moved and a head that told me to fight on, as I'm Welsh after all.

You could say he was winning conclusively on points, using his boxing brain while I used my emotions, to no effect at all. But I couldn't stop going forward, despite being outclassed, so I decided to hit him with a smother tackle.

Bang! To the ground, we both fell and at last I'd stopped the bullets that had already started to sting my face from his bony fists. After we wrestled awhile, I had the cheek to ask, "have you had enough then?"

To which the only logical reply could be, "have you?" We then rolled away from each other and wandered back home.

Within a few days, we were back talking again, as if nothing happened. I learnt a lot that day, which served me well in the future. I learnt that fighting is as much about the brain as brawn, that tactics in a fight, like tactics in life, were important.

Bravery, if you call it that, is pointless if you just charge in without thinking. But most of all, I learnt respect for a boy who taught me a lesson at an early age. A boy who would, to this day, be a friend forever.

That fight seemed to bond us into brothers and throughout our teenage years, we would share countless experiences together as young lads growing up into young men. Then, as we later matured into our twenties, we were inseparable.

I had no idea then, when Alf pummelled my face with his knuckles, that he'd become one of the most influential men in my life.

And so, life went on for boys and girls who, literally, were just boys and girls growing up in the same environment, sharing childhood experiences just like we shared bottles of Corporation pop. We were happy playing on the streets then, not knowing what lay ahead.

Chapter 9
Temptations

As children growing up on the Grove, we were fortunate not to have the temptation of illegal drugs but as time passed, alcohol and girls became an increasing attraction. Dutneys', our corner shop, supplied the Strongbow cider that we all drank as our first tipple, huddled in a circle near the old folk's bungalow.

A few of the girls would join us and I suppose it was at that time that we realised that the girls were different from ourselves. They would happily volunteer for any babysitting jobs, then they'd ask one of the lads to come round to listen to music, often kissing and cuddling to David Bowie songs or Northern Soul music.

Yes, kissing, cuddling and other things we stumbled across those nights, were simply another part of life's education. The next day the boys would meet up, eager to brag if they'd had female company the night before.

In fact, even if they'd not had female company, some would brag as if they had. Often you'd see Glen Rickets, albeit barely fourteen, wave his fingers under the nose of all the other boys, having failed to wash his hands after intimately touching one young girl or another the night before.

Looking back, the smell that Glen shared with us those days after his glorious petting, was many a boy's first sexual experience as a young teenager.

Then, there was lovely Lily Webster. Unlike Suzy Vardy, she didn't seem to target the older boys but rather took pleasure teasing her peers and the younger boys with her presence. As boys, we'd laugh and fantasise about Lily and she knew it.

She surely originated the term of being 'one of the lads', occasionally sharing her mother's sherry or a bottle that she'd stolen from Dutney's. Whatever innocence each of us had in those childhood days, Lily helped us lose some of it.

On one occasion, we rolled out the old Subbuteo pitch in Barry Vardy's front room when his parents were out, a rare time to play indoors without adults arguing. In came Lily, only to find four boys playing a football game on a green velvet pitch, while she wanted to play another game.

Of course, we were taken by her mere presence, wearing a mini skirt and knee-length white boots. Quite an attire for a fifteen-year-old and the sort of attire that demanded that we look up and pay her attention.

But this was a big game we were playing, an FA Cup final between Arsenal and Liverpool and we weren't going to stop for anyone. Or so we thought.

As Lily told us to stop playing children's games, we tried to usher her away, despite the tempting smell of cheap perfume and lipstick. But the more we said, "Lily, fuck off, it's a Cup final," the more she became intent on stealing the whole situation.

Taking one slow step and then another, cigarette between her fingers, she walked on to the green pitch, stamping on the plastic players with no respect at all, before posing in the middle of the pitch, one boot in one half and the other boot in the other half.

There she stood, her legs open wide, laughing at the good of it, while we four boys looked up from the floor, in full view of her knicker-less body. It was a spell-binding image of something that at least two of us had never seen before, an experience boldly thrown at us that we'd never forget.

Then as we admired the sight, Lily leapt out of the room roaring in laughter, having not only broken many of the plastic players but having totally destroyed our concentration. That afternoon, we all realised that the world didn't revolve around football after all.

Despite this, we forgave Lily as she was great fun and we respected her as 'one of the lads'. Even though she preyed on our relative innocence, captivating us like some stunning femme fatal.

Then as time progressed, a couple of the bolder boys chanced their arm with her, while the rest of us continued fantasising. It was Glen Rickets and his older brother, Nobby, who both had romantic flings with Lily while the rest of us looked on, waiting for the train to crash.

Eventually, it was both sad and inevitable to see the two brothers fight it out over Lily's affections, whether she wore knee length boots or not. When two brothers fight for the affections of one temptress, there will never be a winner.

In the course of time, Lily played the field with the two of them, meeting one behind the other's back and vice versa. But such games can only go on for so long. They came to a stop when Glen waved his fingers under Nobby's nose in juvenile pomp, thus alerting his brother to the scent of Lily's recognisable private parts.

Inevitably, the two ended up swapping punches, while the devilish Lily had the last laugh.

Years later, the two brothers eventually buried the hatchet when Glen left the estate to live with his boyfriend, Frank, in Highroad Well. At least he could look back at the experiences with Lily Webster as something that most of us could only dream of.

And maybe his experiences with Lily made him realise the truth about his own sexuality and had enabled him to live happily ever after with the man he loved. However, the fact is that Lily, sweet Lily Webster, taught many boys far more than they ever learnt in school.

Chapter 10
Highlands Grammar School, Early Lessons

There came the time when our experiences living on the Grove estate would be tested in the wider world. Such is the true beauty that education brings. It's not just about opening books and doing homework, it's about opening hearts and minds to a new world.

In doing so, while we learnt lessons to last a lifetime, we inevitably saw our childhood innocence drift away without even knowing it. However, those seven years at Highlands Grammar School were very happy times.

Though it took me months to get over the initial embarrassment of wearing short pants in the first year. Short grey pants on long legs, together with a purple peak cap, made me look like a clown.

But at least we all looked the same and there was no opportunity for one child from a higher income family to stand out and above, from a boy from the local council estate. It was the same when we played sports.

We all had to have the same socks, shorts and shirts for rugby and soccer. We all had to have black pumps for the gym. And we all had to have the same shorts and vests for athletics and basketball.

Each shirt, vest and pair of shorts bearing our initials, as directed by the head of the PE Department, Mr Gibson. My shirts obviously had 'TR' above my heart. Likewise John O'Neill had 'JON' above his heart, which was always handy if anyone forgot his name.

But poor old Niall O'Brien dreaded the 'NOB' that his mummy stitched on to his school kit. In the playground, it was soon elongated to Nobby, an affectionate nickname that he carried through his schooldays up to the time that he died some five years ago.

However, to keep me in the standard kit and uniform wasn't cheap and it came out of mum's purse. Each year, she had to get a fresh loan from the 'Provy man', the weekly door to door collector for Provident Clothing and Loans.

She worked hard to pay all the bills, feed and clothe me and do everything she could to make sure that I never felt disadvantaged while my father didn't contribute anything.

So there I was, a skinny young boy, carrying a leather satchel, Monday to Friday, jumping on the bus from the Grove as it weaved it's way from Ovenden to Illingworth, the brazen, older children sitting upstairs at the back, smoking and bragging to the girls, as teenagers often do.

All in our uniforms, looking like a children's army, marching into registration and the main hall every morning.

I remember that every male teacher wore a tie, a habit that I seemed to follow in my years as a Probation Officer, and they all looked very professional, setting a standard for each pupil to measure up to.

The female teachers were also smart, in that they dressed with the style of classic femininity, as though they were Ingrid Bergman or Audrey Hepburn. Maybe, it was simply an age of smartness and style that we took for granted.

Maybe it was just the high standards that a good school of that era believed in. What those smartly dressed role models taught was enough to pass those essential exams to get me a start in life. But they also taught far more than that.

For example, in those early years at school, we never took much interest in art, apart from the gifted ones who'd probably been etching and sketching with crayons or pencils before they even went to school. But I was like the majority, having no real interest whatsoever.

Until we reached the third form when Mrs Green arrived after the summer holidays. Of course, we had also arrived for the new term, young boys who had miraculously found the early gifts of hormones during those weeks off. Suddenly, we all became budding artists or at least interested in the subject.

Not that we had any talent but sitting in the art class, drooling over Mrs Green, taught us something. Concentration. Even the class bullies, the Richardsons, learnt to focus and say, "Please miss, can I go to the toilet?"

We were young boys totally fixated by a 'real' woman. You could say that our cockles were stirred. In fact, on one occasion, there was more than cockles being stirred.

Each week we looked forward to seeing Mrs Jane Green, for reasons I've mentioned. One day, to show her pupils how classical art can be brought to life in the early '70s, Mrs Green gave us a rare treat. As we sat at our desks at the start of the lesson, she wheeled in a mobile TV set, half a dozen boys jumping up to try and help her.

Then after she introduced the programme to the class, she said those familiar words, "will one of the boys at the back turn the lights off, please?"

As we plunged into total darkness, four of the boys began to whisper so silently that no one towards the front could hear. We later heard that they all agreed to have what they called a 'wanking competition', at the expense of Mrs Green, the subject of their childhood fantasy.

Hidden by the darkness, they camouflaged their seedy actions with occasional coughs, as their favourite teacher whispered praise of Gaugin's Two Tahitian Women, which on reflection, was not the most sensible of paintings to critique with the Richardson twins' et al!

Yet I would wager, to this day, that while Mrs Green would never have known it, she introduced those very boys to a man called Gaugin who used to paint the occasional nude. Education comes in many forms and the unforgettable lessons could be more down to the teacher than the subject.

The girls seemed to be fixated too, coming into the art class with hairstyles trying to mirror that of Mrs Green who they saw as a confident and sophisticated modern woman.

She was one of those teachers that never needed to shout to keep her audience, to get through the work on time, without those arranged delays and diversions that children put into play to pass the day.

Yet, while only a few remained artistically talented, we all learnt the skills of social obedience in her classroom, which was important in life. However, our captivation with the goddess, Mrs Green, seemed to back-fire on the other teachers.

On detention days, a member of staff would have the esteemed honour of supervising the naughty boys and girls who had been given detention for one misdemeanour or another; often smoking, occasionally for fighting and always for any rare backchat to teachers.

Mrs Green, inevitably, never had to put a boy or girl on detention, never had to punish a child by keeping them in after school to do some pointless exercise in total silence. Yet detention, especially when Mr Walton was supervising, was a fearsome experience, let alone a calculated restriction of our liberty after school.

He was a bull of a man, ex-marine, who never flinched when he made us quiver in fear with his cane or his ruler, dispatched as punishment on a bony bottom or a shaking hand.

It was the same when Mrs Lord supervised detention. She was also a product of war time, the rumour being that she was a former spy behind enemy lines, trained to kill with an assassin's smile, before moving into teaching after dropping the nuclear bomb on Japan.

She was mean, hard-faced and hard-voiced but expert at keeping order in the classroom. With Mrs Lord and Mr Walton taking most of the detention classes, there was a fear running through the school, which made every child dread that teacher's call, "Jackson, that's it, Tuesday detention, inform your mother you'll be late for your tea."

But when poor old Mr Walton was off sick with what we hoped were painful piles or terminal loss of speech, Mrs Green stepped in for the next four detentions and of course, as word passed around the school, like nits escaping from the Nit Nurse, detention became very popular.

So popular that all the other teachers, bar our much respected games teacher, Mr Gibson, faced such disciplinary problems in the classroom that detention soon became oversubscribed, mainly by spotty skinned juvenile boys who would walk to Bradford and back for a further sight and smell of Mrs Green.

Boys were doing everything they could to get on Mrs Green's detention list. Nearly every cheeky boy, myself included, broke a rule or two that they'd never previously contemplated doing, as ill-discipline briefly riddled its way through the school.

We were becoming juvenile delinquents by the day. But thankfully for the Headmaster, Mr Walton returned to work within weeks, as fierce and domineering as ever, no doubt his painful piles giving him more appetite for battle in the classroom.

And of course, with Mrs Green no longer a detention supervisor, there was definitely no more reason for randy schoolboys to break the rules.

Chapter 11
'Spare the Rod, Save the Child'

Looking back, I think we remember the fiercest teachers because they made us concentrate and focus during lessons. We had to behave and learn or face the consequences.

Being placed on detention was obviously one consequence of bad behaviour, being sent to the Headmaster's office another and there were other painful consequences that you'd take with a quivering lip because you just couldn't cry in front of other pupils.

Make no mistake, corporal punishment hurt as it was meant to and often it served a purpose. Yet, I don't think that teachers in our school enjoyed dishing out corporal punishment.

I certainly never saw a look of enjoyment or a frenzy of satisfaction on the face of the executioner, when they inflicted the sting of pain and humiliation on a guilty pupil.

In other schools, there were probably a few teachers who did abuse that authority and many children may have been damaged when some teachers overstepped the mark and became school bullies themselves.

But in our school, there was a sense that such discipline was used to educate not harm. We made our mistakes and accepted the consequences.

There are many ways to skin a cat and it seemed that every teacher had more qualities than weaknesses as educators. Otherwise, how would we remember those lessons of life well into our adulthood?

Mr Cooper scared the hell out of us; yet he also entertained us, which takes some doing when you are a physics teacher. He had a body like a block of Sheffield steel, his shoulders being as wide as his full height, his waist as narrow as Mrs Green's.

He was therefore, 'V' shaped but nobody would give this growling teacher the Harvey Smith 'V' sign with two fingers. He'd walk into the room and it would go silent. One summer's day, he walked in and for whatever reason, he called Dougie Smith to the front of the class.

"Come here, Smith," he bellowed, "You're the strongest in your year, aren't you?"

To which Dougie puffed his young, barrel chest out and said, "I am, sir."

Mr Cooper looked young Dougie directly in the eye, them both being the same height of five foot six. "Can you do this, Smith?" he asked as the class encroached the floor in front of the teacher's desk.

Then Mr Cooper lay to the ground before pumping out twenty one-arm press-ups, only breathing gently and comfortably through his nose so as to frighten the class as much to amaze them.

Of course, Dougie tried to follow suit when he was instructed; only to fall flat on his face as his left arm crumpled. The rest of us gasped then laughed, being pleased to see the class bully fall flat on his face for once.

"So, Smith, what have you learnt from that, son?" asked Mr Cooper, as the rest of us listened to hear the right answer.

"That you're stronger than me, sir?" was the reply.

"No, lad, that's not the lesson. The lesson is that there's always somebody smarter than yourself and if I see you bullying anyone else in the playground again, I'll teach you another lesson."

In silence, the class sat down and whatever the ethics of Mr Cooper's teaching on this occasion, it worked and those who had suffered Dougie Smith's bullying before, went home with a lighter heart that night, knowing they weren't alone anymore.

Dave Gibson, our games teacher, was another disciplinarian and for many of us, he transformed our lives in those seven years. He could be tough at times but we knew he cared.

It was he who insisted that we all had the same blue and maroon shirts and vests for sport and spotless white shorts, all carrying initials on the left side no more than an inch high, carefully stitched on by our parents, usually our mothers.

Whether it was in the gym, on the rugby, soccer or cricket pitch or on the running track, we were taught to behave from day one. There was no answering back but he was warm enough to welcome questions at the right time and in the right manner.

There was no ill-discipline on the field of play or in the changing room and it was one rule for everyone, no excuses. He taught us to play by the rules, treat referees with respect, accept their decisions and the decisions of the officials elsewhere.

If you did a 'no jump' in the long jump, as I occasionally did in competition, you accepted the judge's call. "If you get it wrong with your run up, Terry, look at yourself and see what you can do to put it right," he said. "Don't ever look to blame anyone else for your mistakes."

Those words are still lodged in my mind today and I often promoted the same philosophy in my career as a Probation Officer in the years to come.

One day, a boy turned up with dirty white shorts when we were due to play Sowerby Bridge Grammar School in a local derby game. On seeing young 'Stanny' get kitted up, Mr Gibson called him over in the changing room.

"What's this, Stanny? Your mummy always cleans your kit, so what's happened here?"

"I forgot to give it her, sir. I left it in my bag," was the reply.

This resulted in a clipping of Stanny's left ear and the words, "you're a clown lad, you're a clown, get changed, you're not playing today and I'll see you in detention on Tuesday."

Then as we all waited for the order to go on to the soccer pitch, Mr Gibson added the next lesson. "We are a team and we are all going to be well turned out and no individual will let this team down or the school, on or off the pitch. If we look shabby, we will play shabby."

Then, as Tommy Maguire put his kit on to take Stanny's place in the team, he anxiously checked that his own kit was immaculate, as did every other boy in the team. I remember it well.

That was a lesson for us all that afternoon. And there was another lesson learnt the next day. As we played football in the playground at dinner time, Mr Gibson walked over to young Stanny in front of all of his friends.

"How's your mum, Stanny? Did you tell her that I dropped you from the team for not having the right kit?"

"I didn't, sir, was I supposed to?" replied a rather nervous Stanny.

"No, I suppose not but it was up to yourself because it was your mistake and I'm pleased you admitted that to me instead of blaming your mother. So, on reflection, I think I was slightly hard on you yesterday, I sometimes get it wrong. Therefore, I'm cancelling your detention. OK? But you're still a clown, Stanny!"

Then Stanny smiled and thanked Mr Gibson while we laughed loudly at the warmth of it. I'm certain we all saw the lesson there; that lesson being the fairness of a firmly disciplined teacher, who'd reflected overnight to come to the conclusion that he'd been a shade too hard on one of his boys.

It took a good man to do that and an even better man to share it with others as a lesson in life.

Chapter 12
Mr Brown, A Gentle Man,
A Gentle Teacher

In the coming years at school, as I grew out of short pants into long pants, I began to realise one of the most important lessons that we should all take forward in life. That is, we are all different.

Take Mr Brown, for example, our roly-poly figured English teacher. He was chalk and cheese compared to the likes of the hard teachers, like Mr Cooper or Mr Walton. Yet, he was very skilled and evidently a teacher who loved to see children both behave themselves and think for themselves.

I can't recall a bad word, a negative comment, only a warm smile, a forgiving character who knew that education was more than discipline. Looking back, it was obvious that he knew that we were all different, from different worlds. Yet, he taught us to treat everyone with respect or at least he tried to.

Mr Brown never let anyone fall behind in class simply because they were struggling. No one got left behind in his lessons. He'd get you to think about Romeo and Juliet, not just read it out loud. He used to emphasise that everybody can think and speak for themselves.

Whatever our potential or limitations, he wanted us to make the most of ourselves. Looking back, I think he blossomed within the freedom of thought and expression that were alive in the '60s and '70s and he wanted us to be free too.

That included Gavin Hopkins, a shy boy from a difficult family background across the other side of town. A shy pupil who was recently nicknamed Hedgehog, simply because he had his head scalped after being infested with nits.

There were many of us with the same problem, myself included, but none of us had our heads shaved. While he didn't come from Ovenden and was never interested in playing with the boys who were mad into sport, Gavin was a boy from a similar background to myself and Alf. He was harmless, often nervous and always at the back of the class.

As he sat at the back one day, it seemed that Mr Brown realised why he was struggling to participate as much as the other pupils in the class. It wasn't only shyness, it was also because he couldn't see the blackboard from the back of the room.

Yet, when Mr Brown gently encouraged him to sit at the front, in a caring, sensitive way, it merely backfired on both himself and young Gavin. Of course, once Gavin came forward to the front of the class, the usual class bullies began to feed on him until they were stopped.

Every now and again, amid giggles, one of the Richardson twins would throw in a cruel jibe, hoping to disrupt the class at the expense of Gavin and Mr Brown, simply for the sake of their own bored amusement.

"He should be reading Juliet, sir, not Romeo," quipped one of the twins.

While Mr Brown tried his subtle approach to keep order, by saying, "come on boys, focus," this was to no avail. The Richardsons giggled along, trying to undermine Mr Brown by the second and unnerving young Gavin, who sat at the front, his shaved head getting closer to kissing the pages of his Romeo and Juliet book as he bowed his head to hide his blushes.

The Richardson twins took the goodness of Mr Brown as his weakness and were trying to take over the class, with Mr Brown not having the natural aggression to wipe out their bullying at the source. But he had a hidden wisdom that was his secret weapon as well as their undoing.

Group dynamics were powerful. Mr Brown changed tack, to harness the concentration of the Richardsons without taking them on head on. "OK, Montagues and Capulets, were they friends then?"

Of course, this prompted the Richardsons to pipe up because conflict was their sole love, apart from Mrs Green of course. Splitting the class in two, Mr Brown asked one half to go to the coffee room and the other to stay in the classroom.

Bobby Richardson was to lead the Capulets, his brother Ronnie to lead the Montagues. Being given the responsibility to lead was a master stroke. Each group were told to go into their rooms and work out how, if in any way, they could make peace with the other family without losing face.

It was a test of diplomacy, of wisdom. It was a masterful teaching skill in it's own right, getting individuals to work in groups to share perspectives and come up with solutions.

Within half an hour, each Richardson realised their impotency, their own vulnerability, no longer being a twosome who believed that we all wanted to witness their bullying and distraction.

When Bobby was in our group, the Capulets, he was far from the leader, in fact he had to be pushed into expressing an opinion. He simply folded and you could see his control dissipate without his ugly brother and I mean ugly in terms of their shared hostility.

Then Mr Brown joined us, we Capulets, and true to his gentle character, he skilfully pulled Bobby Richardson to the fore of the group, praising him for saying that the Capulets were like his own family who hated another local family, the O'Riordans.

Mr Brown had delivered the trump card, getting two reluctant pupils to identify that they could relate their 1970s lives to those of the Montagues and Capulets. That is what I call teaching that is both the power of the book and the skill of teacher. Who said William Shakespeare was an irrelevant thing of the past?

Mr Brown was perhaps the most skilled teacher I can remember. His force, his engine, was to teach in a manner that befitted his own character. He was true to himself and true to us. His methods worked with kindness.

He was not one of the demanding disciplinarians in the classroom. Rather an honest artist in his craft, who many of us will always remember for his unique ways. For when he pulled the whole class together, to share their perspectives as to how the Capulets and Montagues could live in peace, both Bobbie and Ronnie Richardson for once spoke with sense and maturity on the matter.

The fact is, they were hostile boys at those times when they weren't the class fools, simply because their family life was about conflict and disruption. Like all of us, they were products of their world and their home life was a hard one most of the time.

Mr Brown knew this, he read them like one of his books. He somehow seemed to delve under their skin, never judging a book by it's cover. It was a lesson within a lesson and proved to be somewhat of a turning point in the school career of the resident bullies, the Richardsons.

They would never be angels but splitting them up when they sought to wreak havoc through public bullying, seemed to do the trick. Alone, they faced each one of us and collectively too and when they were encouraged to give their own perspectives on conflict, they were for once, in their element.

The rest of the class had seen their vulnerability and, therefore, welcomed them into the class more than before. After this, I think the twins began to learn that they were individuals with something to offer, not the Kray Twins, born to terrorise.

As for Gavin, a few of us put our arms on his shoulder when we left the classroom. In those days, you didn't hug a boy or a man, nor rarely ask, "are you OK?" But he wasn't alone anymore and he knew it. As did the Richardsons…

Chapter 13
The School Community

When Alf and I went from the world of the Grove, where we'd learnt the local cultures we considered as normality, into the bigger pond of the Grammar School, we saw new worlds for the first time.

Thankfully, I had sport to burn my energy away and to harness my competitive spirit and aggression. So, I suppose I never had the desire to join the Music Society, the Highlands Band or even the Chess Club. Certainly not the Debating Society as the years unfolded.

Though, as Alf recently reminded me, we'd have had to buy our own trumpet or trombone to join the school band and carrying them up and down the Grove in our posh uniforms would have been a health and safety risk in many regards. Looking back, neither of us could have afforded the essential, extra private music sessions, let alone a trumpet or a trombone, although our mothers would no doubt have scrimped and saved or took out more Provident loans if need be.

Our parents certainly couldn't afford to send us on those musical tours to Switzerland or Italy, which seemed to happen each summer holiday for a select band of children.

No, I put all my heart and soul into my sport, my mother making sure that I never went short in terms of kit and appropriate footwear, whether it was for football, rugby, basketball or athletics.

She even bought me cricket whites so that I could play in the cricket team. I spent the whole seven years up to the age of eighteen doing the basics in the classroom whilst enjoying every lesson of Physical Education.

Those were the most magical days. Playing all those sports, up and beyond district and county level by the time I left at 18, I had found my passion in life. In that final year, we reached the Yorkshire Final of the All England Schools Football Association Cup, the semi-final being one of my greatest memories, with all the school cramped around the pitch, cheering us on to victory.

Losing the Final was one of my biggest disappointments in life but Mr Gibson had taught us to take victory and defeat in the same honourable measure. In all our team games, he made us sportsmen as much as athletes, by demanding honesty and discipline on and off the pitch.

The season before that, when I was seventeen, playing for the soccer first eleven, I once went five games without scoring, as centre forwards occasionally do. I turned up for the next game one Saturday morning to be told that I'd been dropped from the team.

I felt humiliated, hurt but Mr Gibson had taught us to just get on with set-backs like this, look at yourself in the mirror and play the game. The familiar message that he taught was that when things start going wrong in life, look at yourself first and don't blame others.

It was a message for the individual and the collective. So, as my first team colleagues played on the top pitch that morning, I briefly looked on in envy from the lower pitch, before getting stuck in to my new situation playing in the reserve team, known affectionately as 'the stiffs'.

Yet we, the second eleven, 'the stiffs', won 9-0 that day and I was lucky enough to score six goals. Mr Gibson had taught me a positive lesson by dropping me and the next week, I was back in the first team, where I remained for that season and the next. I'd learnt to accept my own faults, my own poor performance, without any moaning.

However, for Alf and many others, there was no appetite for sport although every boy and girl had to participate, whatever the activity. In winter, most of us dreaded the cross country run through Illingworth, including the Richardsons, who would nip off the course as it ran past the local shops.

There they'd sneak up to see a girl called Julie, for a quick smoke and a cuddle, before joining the rest of us as we came past on the second and final lap. Mr Gibson never knew that they only ran half the distance of the race because no one was going to grass on the Richardsons.

Then there was Sports Day of course, the highlight of the summer for those who enjoyed track and field athletics. While I and the other athletes participated, the rest of the school looked on, for a while at least.

Many of the spectators seemed to enjoy the sporting entertainment, cheering on individuals or their house teams in the relays. But other supporters, with no interest whatsoever, played their own games while teachers like Mr Walton and Bob Hopkins tried to ensure that those games were soon stamped out.

Some spectators, like the Richardsons of course, used it as an opportunity to sneak off to do some courting with like-minded girls, hiding down the embankment or elsewhere, to kiss and cuddle or to smoke.

Then others, like Alf, played the game of 'Colditz', to try and escape the ring of security formed by the prefects and co-ordinated by Masters Walton and Hopkins.

I've no doubt these two teachers and the specially selected prefects under their orders, thoroughly enjoyed the battle of Colditz, a game so called as children tried to escape home early instead of staying to the end of the sporting day.

Yes, we were all different, all members of a school community in one way or another and I know from speaking to former school friends, that life at the Highlands Grammar School was both a game and a full time education that served us well in the future.

And of course, time passed with some haste, week by week, as you run the race through your teenage years. One day, you're wearing short pants, being lectured to by eighteen-year-old prefects, half of whom are wearing see-through beards or porn-star moustaches, as was the fashion at the time.

The next day, you were thinking about what you should be wearing at the weekends, when the school uniform was hung up for a couple of days.

School was great, because we all had to wear the standard uniform and we all had to turn up for lessons looking relatively smart and conservative in appearance. But when the weekend came, there was the opportunity to find other identities.

Chapter 14
"Ground Control to Major Tom"

I recall the day when four of us, all from the same class, ventured out one Sunday afternoon to Shibden Park to play pitch and putt or bump into girls, before going on to Joe Dawson's house for refreshments.

His mother was a hairdresser and had taught Joe the basic skills in hair care. In those days, most of us were trying to look cool and David Bowie was no cooler guy at the time. I remember all four of us getting silver rinses that day, then each going home our separate ways, half cocky and half embarrassed.

I recall getting a fierce rollicking from my parents before getting told to rinse the colour out of my shoulder length locks. I can never forget my father, laughing amid his rage, "your son's a poofta like his old man," he called out, again insinuating that I was the bastard in the family.

You don't forget those words that easily and on reflection they summed up the cruel and abusive homophobia of the day. But I only wished there was truth in them in terms of him not being my father.

Instead, he was still the man I called 'dad' in the months and years to come and I often still wonder why. By turning up with silver locks, I walked right into his abuse and I only had myself to blame.

I suppose that all four of us thought it was a good idea to try and look cool and peer pressure was important back then. Though maybe my own motivation was to try and embarrass my father after all. I don't know to this day. But, besides all that, there was still the embarrassment of school to come the next morning.

In fact, that morning I would have stayed off sick if I could but that was never going to happen. Mum was, quite rightly, a stickler for education and meeting your responsibilities. So, I went to school, like the other three lads, with strains of silver dye still in my hair, to the constant ridicule of my peers.

The lesson was quickly learnt that trying to be cool was for the cooler boys. In the coming days, things were back to normal, hair wise, but setting yourself up for ridicule among your peers was a big mistake.

In those days, trying to look different by copying pop stars could be a disastrous move as it gave ammunition to others to shout out abuse. If a boy was gay back in those days, he wasn't called gay; he was simply crucified, mentally and often physically.

And if you weren't gay but were called gay in the streets, it was done to both bully you and undermine your developing masculinity. Either way, as I look back, the homophobic taunts that most boys faced at some time or another, were designed to hurt.

Inevitably, it ended in fall outs, even violence. Once again, I walked into a fight simply because of my own inexperience and inability to walk away from the bullying.

Three of the lads in our class, who I thought were my friends, had almighty fun at my expense for a couple of days, calling me a drag queen and throwing other insults, which boys were highly sensitive to.

So, I had no option but to challenge them all to a fight, following which the word got around of 'fight, fight, fight, after school, back of the garages'. There we met up, I and my three adversaries, plus a dozen or so spectators, all desperate to see falling teeth, black eyes and blood or even better, the sight of one boy or another crying.

Such was life and the fight lasted but a few minutes, punches being thrown after head-butts, the usual street entertainment, before a couple of prefects came to either spoil the fun or save someone's humiliation, whilst the crowd booed their arrival. Of course, a couple of the prefects had side bets on the outcome, which was the norm back then.

Then following that, in the coming days, all four of us made up in a cold, gentlemanly manner, recognising that we'd all pitched in to fight, as schoolboys have to do, regardless of potential injury.

The lesson being, it's the taking part that matters, as Olympians say. Plus, of course, pride comes before many a fall. I had no option, whatsoever, than to stand up and defend any reputation I still had after wearing a silver rinse for a few days.

I learnt then that there's no loss of pride if you fight and do your best, even if you limp home bloodied and beaten. But if you walk away in shame, showing a reluctance to stand up for yourself, you've done your worst by doing nothing and if you do nothing in the face of bullying, they know it, you know it and the rest of the world seems to know it too.

Chapter 15
Saturday Afternoons at the Match

One of the lessons that Mr Brown taught in his English Literature classes was that we should all think for ourselves and be ourselves. Unfortunately, as teenagers we often follow the crowd, for a while at least.

On Saturdays in the 1970s, it was customary for most young lads from the estate to follow the fashion of being boot boys, as they were often affectionately termed. There was no call for walking around the Grove, looking like a glam-rock popstar.

That would be a health and safety matter. No, it was a time to wear Ben Sherman shirts, braces, jeans and Doc Marten boots or bomb-proof black brogues, as we went to watch Huddersfield Town.

I guess we were conditioned by the culture that was fostered in that environment at that time. We literally followed the crowds of teenagers and older men, chanting songs of worship or ranting nasty abuse to opposition players and fans. Going to the match on Saturday was the done thing.

I think that most of us secretly dreaded being isolated from fellow supporters going to and from the ground on Leeds Road. There was that sense of vulnerability, that fear of being ambushed by a larger group of opposing supporters, especially when we were young teenagers and they were grown men.

Though it was OK, however, when you were all in a crowd together, protected in numbers and also by police, their horses and barking dogs. You'd chant and swear and verbally abuse the opposing team and their fans; at the same time, hoping that if there was trouble brewing between supporters, it would be short lived, exciting but safe. For most of us, it was a show of bravado just to be in the crowd.

It was a tribal ritual that you wanted to be part of, whilst hoping that you'd come home safely that Saturday evening, to tell the story of how you and the lads chased the Bolton fans into the train station, with fictitious tales of hardness and bravery being told in the following weeks.

For most of us, I guess that the Saturday afternoon ritual was based on fleeting courage and the relief that followed when the day was over. I would never have admitted that back in the day, for obvious reasons, for fear was a dangerous weakness to wear on your shirt.

But for a few, it was their chance to shine in their community, to find legendary status at the price of a criminal record or worse. Yes, I'm convinced that there were a hard core group of fans or thugs that genuinely lived for the violence that was on offer at every game.

Not least a football hooligan called Arnold Dawson. Everywhere he went, he was revered, given celebrity status, everyone calling him by his first name. He'd lead Halifax Town fans into battle, muscles popping out of his muscles, not saying much other than, "come on lads, let's get the bastards," as he rampaged as fast as an eighteen stone muscleman could.

Then later that evening, he'd swan around town centre pubs, people buying him pints as if he was a war hero and nightclub bouncers letting him in for nothing. He'd go straight to the front of the queue, "come on in, Arnie," then spend the evening, quietly flexing his biceps at the bar while younger men looked on in awe.

What was all the fuss about, I wondered, when clubbers often whispered, "Arnie's in tonight." Then, on one boozy Saturday night, I saw two tall, athletic skinheads getting animated in front of old Arnie's face, getting too close for comfort.

Surely no one is trying to intimidate him, trying to make a name for themselves? Then, as the crowd watched on, half in awe, half in fear as to what might happen next, voices raised above the music like heads above war-time trenches.

"Come on then, Arnie, let's have it," said the skinnier skinhead. Within seconds, Arnie lifted one with his left arm and at the same time, he hoisted the other up with his right arm, like lifting balloons.

Together, the two skinheads were in orbit as Suzy Quatro blasted out their screams for mercy, before Arnie banged their heads together like kissing coconuts. As their heads cracked and red juice flowed, he gave them both a swift kick between the legs with his size fourteen Doc Martens; yes, that was what all the fuss was about.

I've never forgotten that brief sight of Arnold Dawson in action and as onlookers clapped for him out of reverence, his legendary status was confirmed again. Over the following days, accounts of Arnie's exploits grew around the town and wider still and I'd be certain that all those who witnessed that example of street justice have never forgotten the experience.

These days, you hear people saying that the term 'legend' is overused. That night, Arnold Dawson; big, soft, loveable Arnie, was a legend in his own small world.

Chapter 16
From Boys to Men

Grandad Parry was an old school headmaster and every summer I had the benefit of his wisdom and Gran's cooking during the long holidays in Wales. It was my annual escape from the estate, from the noisy, dour mills and factories of Halifax in the '60s and '70s.

Those six weeks were blissful. I was a happy child again, away from my father. I learnt much from Grandad, probably because he had so many years' experience watching boys become young men. He was a man of few words. However, two things stick in my mind.

He used to say that 'everybody should learn something every day'. He also said that a boy should never rush to grow up because if he did, he'd make too many mistakes too soon and would therefore never learn.

"Don't be eager to be a fool because you will be anyway," he said. I used to think that was a strange thing to say but now it makes sense.

As our teenage years rolled away faster by the day, some of the boys in school were gathering what we called 'bum fluff' on chins or maybe thin moustaches or side burns. We wanted to look like real men, trying to imitate our sporting heroes.

Though at times, we were unfortunately beginning to look like young porn stars in an age where sexual liberation increasingly threatened the older generation. By then, the more advanced boys were thinking of branching out into public life by going into pubs where our masculinity could be honed and advertised.

Despite my father's alcoholism being the demon in the family, I was no different from the other lads. On Friday nights, we'd get the bus into the town centre to see how many pints of Webster's bitter we could handle. Pocket money was scarce, if anything at all. So, finding part-time work was important.

The school holidays were great opportunities to earn a few quid. I was lucky to get some part-time work at a Christmas tree farm in Ogden when I was sixteen, which was cold, hard work. But it helped me realise that a physical, outdoor career in the frozen north was not my preferred option, regardless of the beautiful setting.

The next year, over the Christmas holiday, I worked as a postman, delivering locally. I enjoyed the experience for what it was, a way to make money so that I could go into town for a night out. I didn't mind walking the streets of Ovenden while humping a heavy bag of letters and parcels around.

It was Christmas after all. And you soon got to know which houses had vicious dogs on patrol in the garden and worse still, on which streets you'd often find loose dogs looking for someone to chase.

I also managed to get a few weeks' work as a gas meter reader that year. It enabled me to buy my first racing dogs, two whippets from the same litter, the legendary Tom and Jason.

Oh, I enjoyed that job and to be fair, I could have settled for that as a career because it was decent money for little effort other than walking the streets and being polite. It had other benefits too, not least in meeting girls.

If you've ever seen the film *Alfie*, you'll realise that every job should have a perk, a spin off. Otherwise, it can be boring. Well, for a young gas meter reader, the perk was the chance to meet girls and women as you wandered around knocking on doors.

It brightened up my day, just to have some banter and occasional flirting. It was through this job that I met a girl called Sue.

I remember it being late one morning as I was going door to door on my rounds. On this particular occasion, I was reading meters in nearby Mixenden when I called at the flat of Becky Sharman, one of the girls in my class at school.

Decked in my Oxford Bags and Brogue shoes, with my Ben Sherman shirt fitting tightly to my skinny frame, I suppose this was the first time Becky had seen me with my real clothes on.

After all, school uniforms never say too much about a boy's personality. Anyway, having read her mum's gas meter, she introduced me to her friend, Sue, at which point I realised that there was more to this job after all.

I was immediately mesmerised by Sue and after a few minutes, I sensed that she might have been at least somewhat interested in me. For whatever reason, she stared at me for an eternity, so much so that I could feel my skin go from light pink to crimson from my neck upwards.

Sue was one of those girls who just looked at you for ages, with a very knowing grin, as though she was planting dirty thoughts into your innocent young mind. Which she did. She then offered to show me her new litter of pups if I called at her flat to read the meter on Friday, an invitation that I accepted amid further embarrassing blushing.

Anyway, Friday came and as I walked up the steps to the flat on the third floor, I pulled out my little green bottle of Brut and as Henry Cooper used to say, I proceeded to 'splash it all over', bellybutton and all.

Running my fingers through my thick locks, I gently knocked on number 16, in nervous anticipation of seeing Sue. No answer. "Don't blush," I kept telling myself as I knocked on the door again.

Eventually, a shadow appeared, coming towards the glass door but I couldn't see for sure that it was Sue. I did notice, however, that whoever was coming to the door had something on their head, maybe a towel.

Then the sublime fell into the ridiculous, as this slender woman opened the door. She was wearing lipstick and thick Dusty Springfield eyeliner, with a towel covering her torso all the way down to her thighs, with another towel acting as a turban.

I was struck by her firm features, not least her bold nose and jutting, square jaw. It was a disturbing sight, a very slender woman wearing make-up that had no chance, whatsoever, of hiding masculine features.

"Well, hello there, what can I do for you, young sir?" she asked as I noticed hands as big as large plates. Caught on the hop, given I was only expecting Sue to be at home, I asked if she was in.

"Who, dear, Sue dear?" she asked.

"Sorry, it's number 16, isn't it?" I asked.

"Yes, dear but there's no one called Sue here, only me dear; will I do?" she asked with a saucy giggle.

"Well, I'm only here to read the meter, that's all."

To which she replied, "Ooh, that's a pity but I haven't had mine read for a long time, love, so come on in. Coffee?"

Suffering some more blushes, I read the woman's meter after which she asked, "so, do you have a girlfriend then or don't you bother?"

It was the 'or don't you bother' bit that unnerved me. I then blushed more and more, from my collar to my scalp, waiting for my hair to set on fire, before making my way to Becky Sharman's flat so as to ask where the hell Sue was.

"I'm sorry I can't ask you in, Terry," she said, "Father Patrick has called to see my mother."

"That's fine," I replied, sensing that the fool in me had been just as exposed as the scantily dressed woman that I'd just met at number 16. "But I called at Sue's, at number 16 and there was this lady there with no sign of Sue."

"Oh," Becky replied, "why did you go to number 16? Billy Brown lives at number 16. Did you read his meter, Terry?" she asked with a knowing laugh.

I shook my head, saying nothing, knowing full well that the joke was on me, especially when I left the flats hearing roars of laughter above, none of which sounded like a priest called Patrick.

I soon realised that a teenage boy who thinks he can behave like a man, is easy prey to be ridiculed by much more mature young women. I also realised that I'd have to do something about that blushing.

I had a lot to learn, regardless of how much Brut I splashed on my torso and other parts of my young body. How I thought that Sue would even be interested in me, I'll never know. I should have known that I was out of my depth.

Sue and Becky taught me a lesson in the dangers of an inflated ego, just like Alf taught me a lesson in boxing some years earlier. They set me up, made a fool of me, though I knew then that there was only one person to blame and that was myself and my own gullibility.

As Mr Gibson kept telling us, when things go wrong, look at yourself first before blaming anyone else. I'd learn from it but in the many years to come, it certainly hindered my self-confidence.

I'd realised as a teenager that most boys, even the Richardsons and certainly Alf, were much better in 'chatting up' girls than I was. But I just about got by in that regard, despite my shattered nerves, when the courting net spread to Halifax town centre.

Chapter 17
Lessons in Love

At one time in the '70s, Halifax was described as the night out 'capital of the north'. Even coachloads of Geordie girls would come down from Newcastle and you'd often hear them in the Plummet Line or Lewins, "and what's your name, canny lad?"

Then, of course, we'd pick up some of their dialect, being introduced to terms like 'spring chicken' and 'a tidy boiler'. At weekends Alf and I were as thick as thieves, young lads venturing into the town centre, going from pub to pub in search of female company while hundreds of others did the same.

But my nerves always got the better of me in those days, as I struggled to introduce myself to any female without having had a few pints to calm me down. Underneath, I was blatantly shy and I knew it, though I tried to hide it.

I would spot an attractive woman across the room but would never have the courage to walk over and talk to her.

But I learnt, like we all learn, that there's great enjoyment in being young, free and hopeful, however shy we are. 'Nothing ventured, nothing gained' should have been my motto, as I realised the fear of rejection is shared by others too.

I soon had my own little courting spot in the town centre, down the doorway to Wilberforts' shop. It was hidden somewhat from passers-by and regularly used for kissing and cuddling and occasionally a bit more.

Of course, I was never in a position to take girls back home. After all, why would I introduce anyone to my father? Knowing him he'd either make a pass at them or he'd sit in his grubby chair and wet his pants.

But when I met Jenny that changed. It didn't take me long to realise that she was as special as much as she was beautiful. We met on a day out to Filey and we were together for the next three years.

I took her home to meet my mother, who no doubt primed the old man by telling him how to behave in her company. And he did behave, possibly out of respect for her but also because he liked her feisty character.

Jenny loved my two whippets and I think my father liked that. Plus the fact that Jenny was just a good, honest, working class girl, with a strong sense of humour who looked like Rita Hayworth, according to the old man.

In fact, it was through Jenny that I had my one and only memory of my parents having a night out together. That night was special. I saw my old man dance and boy, could he dance. Watching him with mum was something I remember to this day, as they were rocking and sliding around the dance floor as though it was years earlier in the wartime.

I remember looking on and being in disbelief as they drew the crowd's attention with their dancing. Then he danced with Jenny's mum between chatting away with her father, Wilf, about 'men's stuff'; no doubt racing and rugby.

For once, I saw him in a different light, one which made me understand why he was popular with those he used to socialise with. But that was the only time that I saw them out together in my whole life.

For a few hours, he turned the clock back and for all the troubles they had shared at home, they looked like a couple. In fact, those few hours made me realise that mum had been reminded, albeit very briefly, why she fell for him in the first place all those years ago.

It was as though my dad, from somewhere, had turned the clock back to reveal a man who wasn't the monster that I'd learnt to live with.

But the night wore on and, eventually, the drink took its toll. When the three of us arrived back home that night, it was a relief to get him back to his bed before another war broke out. The next day, he was back to his usual self, pestering then bullying mum for money to drink, then home again to wet the bed.

Who could have blamed my mother if she'd left him, given that one night of happiness in the public eye was a very rare experience?

As for myself and Jenny, I suppose it was bound to end sooner or later, despite thinking that we were each other's first love. It's part of growing up and just another lesson in life. In fact, I soon learnt another lesson as to both gullibility and trust.

I managed to get Jenny a part-time job working in a local pub, some months after I'd done the same for one of my mates at school, George Dennis. I thought that I was helping them both out, giving them the chance to earn a few quid working in a town centre pub.

But it backfired when I heard rumours that Jenny and George had been sharing more than the same shift on Friday evenings. I put two and two together, coming up with four, as you would.

Strong men can make their own minds up, I told myself, before deciding to ignore any protestations from Jenny. Getting your heart broken this way and at the same time being made to look a fool by both of them, wasn't good for an ego that had previously been seriously damaged by Becky's friend, Sue!

So, I let them both know what I thought of their treachery, before going home to discreetly lick my wounds over the next weeks. At times like that, you don't advertise your stupidity nor do you put your injured pride out there for everyone to see.

During the following weeks, Jenny tried to make amends but my pride was hurt, having been let down by two friends in the same, sordid instance. After a few weeks of trying to resurrect the relationship, Jenny said she'd be going to work in Italy if I didn't want to be in a relationship with her.

Of course, I did still want her but pride is always more important than shame, so I just had to get on with my life. So, off she went to Ischia with her friend, Jane, and life went on. I reminded myself that I'd been partly to blame for the demise in our relationship because I threw them together in the first place.

I had done this out of innocence and trust, believing that they were both friends that I could rely on. I was now beginning to realise that life wasn't so straightforward, even among friends.

Life went on for Jenny in Italy, though she kept writing to me in hope that we'd get back together on her return. When she came home some months later, I was happily involved with Helen Gailbraith, a farmer's daughter from Ripponden.

We'd become close and she'd helped me move on from Jenny. But then, it was time for another lesson. On coming back to town, Jenny wanted to reignite our relationship and to be honest, it was an appealing proposition.

But it was the wrong thing to do as I was with Helen now. This time it wasn't just pride at the centre of my thinking. It was the realisation that my relationship with Helen mattered and that deserved to be respected.

In the following weeks I would occasionally go into town and on one occasion I bumped into Jenny when I was on a night out with Alf. She was aware of Helen but said that we needed to talk, to finish things properly and to finally leave on good terms.

The next day, we met in town for a coffee and for some stupid reason, I invited her to a friend's flat to talk things over. There we talked and reminisced about some wonderful times and it was obvious there was a flame still there for both of us.

The afternoon passed with inevitable consequences but we both soon agreed that it was a mistake, the wrong thing to do because I was still with Helen. So, now all my talk of pride and doing the right thing by Helen was only self-political nonsense. I'd told myself that Helen and our relationship mattered, yet I was too weak to honour that claim.

A week later, I made the mistake of agreeing to have a night in the town centre with Helen. I remember her pretty face, short blond hair and long skinny legs as she wore that shiny red jacket, as she often did. She was a lovely girl.

We walked through the town centre, going down one of the underground tunnels, only to bump into a lively bunch of young women walking towards us, Jenny being the loudest. "So, Terry, how are you? I take it this is Helen?"

After which I nodded and said, "yes and Helen, this is Jenny." It was no time to have a happy reunion, so I politely started to move off, only to hear Jenny shout back towards Helen and myself.

"You need to watch him, love; ask him what he was doing with me last week."

Of course, Helen did ask me as I tried to calm her down. She was no fool by any means, the only fool was me. This time, my blushing was the blush of guilt and there comes a time when you cannot deny the truth, however embarrassing or painful.

As Helen cursed me, as only a farmer's daughter can, she launched her red handbag to my jaw, then jumped into a taxi never to be seen again. That night, I learnt the two sides of love.

The innocence of Helen compared to the cruelty of my own desire, knowing full well that the latter was totally down to my own weakness.

I look back at that time in dark shame, for my lack of self-control and lack of respect. There wasn't much difference between me and my father after all. He might have used control and violence in his life while I made an absolute point of not following in his footsteps in that regard.

But the lack of respect I saw him show my mother was barely different than the lack of respect I'd shown Jenny and more significantly, Helen, at that time. As my old teacher, Mr Gibson used to say, look at yourself when it all goes wrong.

If you do that and look long and hard enough, you might learn the lesson. The loss of two good friends, Jenny and Helen, was ultimately down to myself alone. From that shameful experience, I felt an emotional loss which changed my thinking forever.

My own shallow weakness was my responsibility, regardless of the fact that I believed Jenny, at that time, had cheated on me. Hurting people through neglect or intent may be different in process but the result is similar.

My mother's experiences taught me that you had to protect and respect people. My father's mother, Nain Roberts, used to always say the same thing to me when I visited her in North Wales when I was a young boy.

"Be a good boy, always look after your Mam," then "don't turn out like your father." Powerful words from a wise old lady living in her old stone cottage, careful to tell her grandson never to hurt women like her own son had done for all those years.

And while I know that I have never physically hurt or controlled any woman in my life, I do know that the hurt I caused Helen and Jenny was through my lack of consideration and the choices I made.

It's easy to say, on reflection, that we all make mistakes. True. But that is no excuse when others suffer. What bothers me now, is that a few years later, I discovered that my assumption that Jenny had cheated on me in the first place was based on quicksand and not concrete fact.

Yes, I got it totally wrong all those years ago when I assumed the worst that Jenny had cheated on me by sleeping with George. That assumption, at that time, was totally wrong.

But it made me mistrust relationships to the point that I've always believed that they die sooner or later.

While love may be like an orange, with two halves made for each other, the orange eventually rots away. That belief has done me no good and I know it now.

Chapter 18
Leaving Home for the First Time

Yet life went on and I had to think of my future beyond school life, beyond Jenny and Helen. By the time I was eighteen, having failed to secure work as a trainee journalist, I decided to apply to go to college.

I had no realistic aspirations in terms of a career bar journalism, so I took the Deputy Headmaster's advice to enter further education. Mr O'Brien said that you'd need a degree to boil an egg in the future, so I took him at his word.

But there was no plan, other than to try and enjoy college sport and, hopefully, find a career along the way. It pleased mum too, as she believed that it would help me find a suitable position in life, with security and respectability.

I knew that helping her son find a decent career was high on her wish list and always had been. But leaving home at that time was not a clear-cut decision.

Yet, despite any doubts I had about going to college, my mother also wanted me out of the house so that the domestic violence didn't become a domestic homicide. On one occasion, as I and the old man wrestled in the back garden like two bears with toothache, she screamed for us to stop.

She then took me to one side and said that whatever she had been through or would go through again, she didn't want me ruining my life by killing my father, intentionally or not. I can hear her words now, pleading with me to move on in life, knowing full well that one day either her husband or her son would get seriously hurt.

Once again, although she was trapped in a cruel, abusive relationship, she was always thinking of others. "We've come too far," I remember her saying. She didn't want that nightmare that we'd shared through all those years to be in vain.

So, I decided to leave the estate for the first time because staying there would probably have been a disaster, sooner or later.

I left the Grove behind me in mid-October 1976. I travelled to Lampeter University, eyeing the Welsh countryside as it crept into the deep western part of the country of my birth. I felt like I was going home.

I eventually arrived in the market town of Lampeter. It was a far distant cry from the streets of industrial West Yorkshire but like a good student, I did my best to settle into student life.

I met many good people there in that first year, mainly through sport and the socialising that flowed from that. I also met Sandra Davies.

She was a Welsh trainee nurse who would occasionally sneak me into the nurse's quarters for late night suppers and to help her with her exam revision. She used to say that she needed to use my naked body as a specimen to remind her of those fundamental male parts that every nurse needed to be acquainted with.

And I was only too happy to help because education is a beautiful thing that should be shared. Well, the justification for lying stripped naked on a bed to be explored sensually by a beautiful young nurse in uniform was too much of a public service to deny.

It really was a form of community service, I told myself, as she asked one question after another. "So if I play with these, will it help the patient relax and improve their mental health?" Or, "shall we try that again to see how quickly the main organ can recover from the first presentation?"

She was a saucy woman, in the nicest sense of the word and she made my stay in Lampeter an educationally rounded one. After all, I'd learnt from my schooldays that education comes in all disguises and it should always be received and shared graciously, in the best interests of the student and also the teacher.

Yet, despite the heavenly distractions of Sandra Davies, it didn't take me long to realise that I was in the wrong place at the wrong time. I enjoyed my studies, those being History, Philosophy and English Literature.

The debates over the existence of God fascinated me and I began to see things with more logic and reasoning. And I loved playing for the University soccer team and the socialising that came with it.

But there was always a cloud hanging over me, the worry about what was happening back home with my mother and father. I was in the dark, distracting myself through college life and all that entailed.

Remember, in those days communication was poor for most of us. There were no mobile phones and my parents never had a phone in the house. I soon realised that I was making the most of my situation whilst trying not to worry about what was happening in Yorkshire.

It didn't take me long to realise that I could never justify staying at Lampeter for another two years, given that my heart and thoughts were elsewhere. I travelled back to Yorkshire three times that year to play for Ogden Athletic, whilst taking the opportunity to see my mother.

But it was not enough, it merely reinforced my concerns as to how my mother was managing to live safely with the old man. So, on passing my first year exams, I said goodbye to good friends and returned to the real world.

By that time, Sandra and I had drifted apart, as lovers often do, though we drifted away with smiles and happy memories. I guess she needed other male specimens to explore and learn from and I couldn't blame her for that.

We were young after all. She was one orange of love in my life that never went rotten.

Chapter 19
The Pursuit of Freedom

When I returned to Yorkshire, I had two intentions. First, to ensure that my mother was safe and eventually free and secondly, to find work. I was a working class lad after all. Initially, I stayed with my parents but that didn't last long because my relationship with my father was as low as it had always been.

I had nothing but contempt for the way that he treated my mother and it was obvious that he'd learnt nothing in this regard while I'd been away. I'm certain that he had no regard for me either, making it quite clear that I wasn't welcome in the family home anymore.

I was also the one who came from a different era, a new generation which he refused to accept. He had given his best years to fighting a war for freedom, returning home to work on damp building sites whilst being increasingly in the grip of alcoholism.

He resented the opportunities of modern youth, given that he had given his own best years for little reward. He hated the new freedoms of sexual liberation but I've no doubt that he'd had his fair share of adulterous relationships over the years. I know he had a daughter who lived in Goole, though this never came to light until after his death.

Fundamentally, we were more than generations apart. Whenever there was a film on at home and the old man was sober enough to watch it, as soon as any kissing and cuddling flashed on to the screen, he'd turn it off immediately, with his usual outburst of, "why do they spoil a bloody good film with that nonsense?"

Yes, anything that reminded my father that there was a younger generation who had a passion for life really irritated him. He even hated the look that many of us had, the brightly coloured shirts, the long hair, the coloured shoes and kidney shaped collars.

He hated the fact that National Service had finished and that people had the opportunity to go to nightclubs while others were in the forces serving their country. He often said that the younger generation had too much choice and too much freedom for their own good.

He hated the opportunities that our generation had to go off to college and their right to express unconventional opinions. As for any youth who didn't walk and talk like a man, he was surely 'a poofta'.

He often said he was a God-fearing man, adding that the younger generation had no moral fibre. What a hypocrite! In fact, I never saw him show any interest in anyone in the younger generation, other than Jenny, simply considering the rest of us to be layabouts who 'never had it so good'.

Put mildly, he had opinions that were brutally blinkered and which made him into a 'grumpy old git', as I often called him.

So, I soon moved in with Alf. He'd bought a small terraced house just off Queens Road, as much to leave the Grove behind as to put down fresh roots. He had a hard life living with his father following his mother's death when he was fifteen.

As for myself, I'd found a steady job, one that mum was delighted with, as a Town Planning Technician with the local council. Her own job was done in terms of rearing me, buying my school uniforms and helping with my education.

She could see that through my growing independence and now it was time for her to focus on herself when the reality of her pending retirement came to light.

Retirement would mean less regular income and a small lump sum, which my father would soon steal away for his own selfish needs. Then, when her pension was finally gone, who would pay the bills and put food on the table?

The old man had never done any of that in the past, so why would he do so in the future? Her life would be even more unbearable once she retired because my mother would be worthless to my father, day by torrid day, week by hopeless week.

If he couldn't scrounge his drink and cigarettes and gambling money off her, what use would she be to him? It was a disturbingly frank and logical question that she'd have to answer before it was too late.

Then the day came. I remember meeting her at a café down Woolshops one dinnertime, as we sat eating our usual treat of sausages, chips and gravy, with a large white mug of strong, sugary tea.

"Mum, now is your chance," I said. Then we discussed the great escape, the one and only ever opportunity that she would have to find freedom. At last, despite all the conditioning that she had suffered, her heart and mind opened up to a dream.

As I write this, I can remember my own forever sense of that moment and I can picture my mother's tears as it finally hit her that she could escape. I managed to convince her that if she did not escape on the day that she retired, my father would kill her, deliberately or not.

Old Dr Hyland, our kind and considerate GP, had told her that she might not survive continuing violence and the violence was certainly continuing, as was my father's psychological control. If she stayed with my father after retirement, her life would be both miserable and short-lived.

The following week, an appointment was arranged with a solicitor on Harrison Road. Whatever the solicitor's fees were, I don't know. But they were the best pounds and pennies that ever left my mother's purse.

The solicitor must have heard the same old stories time and time again, of divorce applications due to 'unreasonable behaviour' or adultery and if only we could prove the latter, life would have been far easier.

No, it was either the hard way or no way to liberation, as he asked my mother for ten examples of unreasonable behaviour. To which mum simply couldn't reply at all, clamming up in a fog of memory loss, no doubt because there were so many examples to choose from.

She was being asked to recall and give insight to a bastard marriage, one with no warmth or security, one that only constrained and choked her like a boa constructor. One that persistently made her question herself; after all, if his behaviour was so 'unreasonable', why didn't you leave him?

She later told me that looking for those ten examples of unreasonable behaviour was like being told to justify her own behaviour. Such is the psychological damage of long term abuse, when the victim is conditioned by the offender to believe that she is the problem; so, how on earth can she tell a complete stranger that her husband is responsible?

Thankfully, the solicitor allowed me to help and so I did as carefully as I could, knowing that the evidence was crucial for the escape plan to succeed. I reminded mum of many incidents, some hidden just below the surface, others deeper.

That was always going to be the case because the only way she survived such traumas was to bury them. The pulling of her hair as he dragged her around the room. The punches to her body and her face, the stitches that marked the spot.

The brain haemorrhage, the scar and dented skull that Dr Hyland believed was down to his violence. The urinating in the bed and in the chair, the constant demands and threats for money.

The indignity suffered when he called to her place of work drunk, likewise the humiliation he inflicted in public, shouting at her in the street and on the bus, the total belittlement by one man on one woman.

His total failure to contribute financially, in any regard, year after year. The control he placed on her to the point that she had to hide any friendships and couldn't go anywhere without his permission.

The culture of fear, violence and control that grew like a cancer inside the family home, which not only put his wife at risk but also his son. He was responsible for all this and more, year in, year out, all of which you had to keep secret because people would inevitably ask, " but why put up with it?"

After that appointment with the solicitor, mum returned home as quiet as a mouse, never uttering a word to my father. There was time for the truth at a later, safer, date. As the solicitor prepared the case, in full knowledge of my mother's plan to escape on her retirement, the world went on with my father having no idea what was rumbling underground in his life.

Then the day came. After leaving work for the last time, she flew off to Johannesburg to stay with Auntie Beryl and Uncle Ron. The day she left on that plane will always be the best day of my life because I knew that the next time I would see my mother, she would be divorced and free.

I can remember my father asking where she was, assuming that she may have gone to North Wales to stay. I took the greatest pleasure in enlightening him as best I could, knowing that this was one part of my mother's life that he couldn't control.

"I don't know," I said, "but you need to get used to looking after yourself because your marriage is over. You've brought it on yourself." As he cursed and called me a bastard for the umpteenth time, I left him to it.

As I closed the door behind me, I heard him ranting, "she'll be back, she'll be back."

Then in the coming weeks and months, my mother began to realise that her freedom was beginning to be regained in the summer Springbok sun, safe with those who would protect her.

As the divorce began to run it's course, the reality began to hit home to my father but when I visited him again, at mum's request, he still wouldn't accept it. Again, I made it clear that it was 'chickens coming home to roost', that he'd brought it on himself.

Why would she work all her life to look after an abusive man and then decide to spend all her retirement with him, as he swindled and dwindled away any little pension that she had earned over the years?

Why would she continue to put her physical and mental health at risk to stay with a brute of a man who never did what a loving husband would do, that is, show love and respect? How many times should a wife share a wet bed and a bed for whatever purpose other than to satisfy the beast?

Like a barbaric man who kept a beautiful caged animal, he could not accept that the cage was no longer locked and that the beautiful creature had silently escaped to find freedom.

That in itself, that escape, is my own definition of freedom in life. That right to go where you want and live how you want to without harming others. Even now, when I need to love myself in times of difficulty, I just look back at that escape to freedom and remind myself that I did one thing in life that really mattered.

After surviving years of domestic violence together, I helped my mother regain her freedom at the age of sixty, after which she would find twenty-five years of happiness.

In the months following the divorce, I had hoped that my father would become used to the idea of his new life. In some ways he did, surprisingly managing domestically, whilst always thinking that one day she'd be back, despite the divorce.

Brother Ronnie also rammed home the fact that the marriage was over and I'll always remember him saying to the old man, "that's two lives that you've tried to ruin, you deserve all you get."

Ronnie's mother, Winnie, suffered the same experiences of domestic violence from our mutual father before she died of cancer and Ronnie was never going to play soft hearts with the old man. Neither of us were. But then one day, the old man silently disappeared and the alarm bells exploded.

By this time, mum had returned from South Africa to stay with John and Amanda in Denbigh, North Wales, retired and divorced. She was to stay there until she felt strong enough to move into her own house.

Then from out of the blue, I heard via Ronnie, that my father had visited our Uncle John in Ruthin, only nine miles from Denbigh. He'd gone to see my Uncle John, no doubt to play the injured brother whose wife had left him high and dry.

Though I know from speaking to my Uncle John many years later, that sympathy from his brother was the last thing my father would get. The rest of the Roberts family in Ruthin knew my father all too well and the only surprise was that the marriage had lasted so long in the first place.

However, later that afternoon while at work, I received a call from Amanda to say that my father had arrived in Denbigh, asking to speak to mum. Here he was turning back the clock, the predator chasing down the woman he'd held captive over all those married years.

Here he was knocking on the door of a woman, his step daughter Amanda, who had refused to live with him when she was an eight-year-old girl, simply because she knew the badness in him.

Yes, a young girl who feared him to the point that she could never live with him even though this meant she could also never grow up with her own loving mother and her younger brother. That decision my sister Amanda made tells you everything about the brute of a man my father was.

Yet he turned up like poison in an old wound, bringing nothing with him but bad news. Though this time, there was no going back for my mother. The strength and shelter she had that day, from John and Amanda, was the very end of my father's control over her.

John was the most honest, solid protector in every sense, with a strength of character that would never be intimidated by my father or any man for that matter. I have no doubt that whatever little conversation there was, it lasted long enough for my father to turn tail and walk away.

On hearing the story, I knew again that my mother's future was safe back home with John, Amanda and the rest of the family in Denbigh.

When my father returned to the Grove, I knew that I had to lay down my own marker, to make sure that he never harassed my mother again. Before calling up to the house, I rang mum at Amanda's.

She assured me that she was safe, in body, soul and mind. Her life was ahead of her again, after all these years of entrapment. I told her that I was going to see my father that day, to reinforce the message and to tell him that I would never be seeing him again. It was over.

I honestly thought that this would further help and protect my mother but her response that day would never be forgotten. As I cursed him for chasing her down and told her to grasp the years of freedom ahead, she pulled me up and spoke to me like only a mother can.

She firmly put me in my place, saying, "he's your father, whatever he's done, never forget that." After everything that she had been through, she still insisted that I never turn my back on him for good.

I will never totally understand how she could show such concern for him, especially after all that she'd been through. But I gave her my word, though I did say I would visit him and give him an ultimatum as to his future conduct.

Consequently, a few days later I told him that I was ashamed of him for upsetting my mother by seeking her out. It was over and he had to accept that. I also said that if he ever wanted to speak to me in the future, if he ever wanted to have any contact with me at all, that would stop immediately and forever if he ever made any contact with my mother again.

He gave no reply to that, no promises. Just a cold, blue-eyed, intense look of acceptance. I walked away, the truth having been told and having put the responsibility on my father's shoulders, where it should always have been.

That night, knowing that my mother's hell was over, I knew I had done the right thing. Mum had left the estate and finally left her abuse behind her. The physical scars would remain but would never be repeated.

As for the mental and emotional scars, they would never disappear for good, despite being buried away.

Chapter 20
Red Bricks and Loose Dogs, Never to Be Forgotten

I didn't visit my father for some time but I did go back when Ronnie moved in. While I had promised my mother that I'd never turn my back on him for good, I was in no rush to see the old man.

Besides, now that mum had escaped, it was time for me to sort my own life out, away from the Grove and old habits. It was time to kick on, in terms of becoming a working man. My job as a Town Planning Technician was steady but uninspiring and I felt I was simply treading water for too long; no plans, no ambitions.

My old PE teacher from school, Mr Gibson, once again came into my life with words of wisdom that I remember to this day. I'll come on to that shortly but in terms of regaining contact with my father, I eventually decided to visit him.

I remember his face to this day, not one of a merry welcome, just a blunt "oh, it's you." He was still living on the Grove estate, having moved just around the corner to Athol Gardens after some local authority housing improvements.

Thanks to my mother, the rent had always been paid on time and this allowed the sitting tenant to buy the property.

My brother Ronnie saw the opportunity to buy the house at a knock-down price and so took the brave decision to move in with the old man.

Of course, it would be in Ronnie's name, as he was in established work as a mechanic in Huddersfield. He was sharp enough to see the opportunity to buy the house and it made sense to do so. So, there they were, the Roberts' family, a not-so-happy, highly dysfunctional family again, living on the Grove estate.

Well, I suppose they were as happy as it could have been given the circumstances. Dad knew that I'd orchestrated mum's escape, along with Amanda, but that was never mentioned when I made that first visit back.

It was good to see Ronnie settled in with the old man and his son Gareth, who had this great affection for my father. He seemed to look up to him as a likeable rogue, a heavy drinker and gambler who enjoyed the craic and who was popular among other like-minded men.

But of course, young Gareth never had first-hand experience of what my father was really like; though his father, Ronnie, often told him never to take his grandad's affability and roguish humour at face value.

Ronnie and I both knew, through both our mother's suffering, that he was cruel and controlling, the furthest thing from a decent family man. Yet the three of them, my dad, brother Ronnie and young Gareth, made the best of things.

Though I often heard that my brother would understandably curse our father for his behaviour, threatening to kick him out and make him homeless for 'living like an animal', as Ronnie put it.

Dad still had a massive drinking problem, occasionally wetting the chair and carpet and once he almost set the house on fire by smoking in bed when he was legless and thoughtless.

Then there was the time when Ronnie gave him cash to buy the weekend meat for the three of them, only to hear the old man say that he'd left the large parcel of beef and mince in a local pub, claiming it must have been stolen.

Of course, the truth came out when one of the old boys in the Shakespeare spilled the beans. Because our drunken father never had the meat stolen at all; in fact, he'd never even bought it!

As usual that lunchtime, Paddy O'Byrne had wandered into the pub selling parcels of meat at knock-down prices to the regulars.

On this occasion, my father declined Paddy's offer of cheap grub in front of his cronies, before putting all the money on an odds-on favourite that the landlord, Hoppy O'Neill, said was unbeatable. You can guess the rest and the next day it was egg and chips for Sunday dinner.

Then there was the time when dad came home drunk and started to cook one of his legendary fry-ups in well over an inch of dirty cooking lard, only then to set the nearby chip pan on fire as he fell asleep in his chair before young Gareth called the fire brigade.

Dad was a nightmare to live with because of his drinking and Ronnie was very patient with him. Far more than I could have been. Then as time passed, having grown from boy to man, in later years I'd meet my father once every couple of months for a quiet pint after Ronnie finished work on Saturday lunchtime.

I did it as much out of duty as I could never forget or forgive him. Mum would often ask, "Have you seen your father?" and when I said I had met him for a pint with Ronnie, it clearly pleased her.

As for herself, in all the years that followed their divorce, my mother met him once more before he died. It was when she came to visit when I was living with Fran in Cleckheaton. Mum wanted to see him because she knew he was very ill.

But she couldn't bear to go and see him at home, in Athol Gardens, save the fear of bringing back too many memories of our life up the Grove. So, I took her into Halifax that Saturday and we went into the Shakespeare.

After one drink together, I left the two of them to have time alone. I don't know what was said but I'm glad they said it. The fact was that mum met him with a smile, just as she wanted to and she left him with a silent tear in her eye.

She told me later that she was glad that she had the chance to see him one last time and anything that remotely made my mother happy was the most important thing as far as I'm concerned. My father died some months afterwards.

I used to go and see him regularly, both in hospital and in the hospice. I went every day in the final weeks and was there when he died that night. This time, I was there not just out of duty but also sadness.

If only things would have been different all those years ago. Looking back now, I think some of my mother's compassion had eventually passed on to myself.

Chapter 21
Days Never to Forget

There is a saying, that 'you can take the lad out of the estate but you can't take the estate out of the lad'. Maybe there is some truth in that.

When Father Jim wrote to me, I think he was trying to say that it is the responsibility of every person to find their own personal truths, not to ignore them, nor to expect somebody else to wave them away as mere consequences of life itself.

His words inspired me to take a look at myself, at my life, to see if it makes sense after all. I was curious to see where I really came from, in terms of the environment and experiences that were almost lost in time. I think that I was looking for myself, hidden in the past, to get some hope for the future. Had my journey in life been worthwhile? For when we die, the only person who can really tell the truth dies too. At least these words, of a very ordinary man, are now in black and white rather than forgotten or buried forever.

Treading any minefield is dangerous for obvious reasons but coming through it safely can be a wonderful thing. I took that risk and questioned many of the events of my early years, recalling days gone by and the people I shared them with.

Of course, some of those people have passed away now and, therefore, some of their names have been changed to protect reputations they cannot defend. I owe those people, those times, so much.

In that vast estate of red brick houses, where loose dogs roamed, life was not easy, nor pretty and never comfortable. We had nothing but each other, inside houses and on the streets, living in each other's pockets and sometimes picking each other's pockets.

At times, it was harsh and uncomfortable but it was our life, nonetheless. The concrete and bricks piled upon each other into the distance and beyond, almost entombing lives of those who lived there.

Was it built to house us or to contain us? It certainly wasn't designed to inspire but it was our home. One to be proud of, when people outside often mocked those who 'lived up the Grove'. That is how it felt at times.

But it built gritty Yorkshire character, as people worked in mills and factories or on building sites. Or didn't work at all. People lived from weekend to weekend, often with Working Men's Clubs and pubs bringing them together just like bank holidays to Scarborough and Blackpool.

Then the television set played an increasing role in our lives, showing us how the other half lived and reminding us, through Coronation Street, that we were not alone in our northern existence.

And we drifted away, watching sport on the 'tele', getting home early to watch Match of the Day before some drunks fought outside the Noah's Ark pub, on cobbles that never mopped up the blood.

Then, of course, there were family squabbles and fights, in most homes on many nights, nearly always fuelled by drink and frustration. But life went on, week by week, when nothing changed and barely anyone escaped the simple world we knew.

Yet looking back, this world where outsiders would rarely venture into, also had it's hidden beauty, which I can see now even if I couldn't see then. After all, there is something extremely beautiful and powerful about resilience in a very ordinary life, a resilience that helps you survive and learn so as to have a better future.

I thank my mother for that, for her resilience has been my inspiration. I hope that others can look back into their own troubled past and see where their own goodness and resilience came from because finding that can be uplifting and inspirational. The answers are there in everyone's personal minefield, if you are brave enough to search for the truth.

For all our dysfunction and fights, there was humour and there were characters to last a lifetime. As there were no stars to guide us, we looked to our local heroes, who were often heroines, though we never considered them as such at that time.

They were often mothers who brought up children amid the scourge of domestic violence and economic hardship. Sometimes, they were fathers who were heroes in the war then forgotten and lost souls afterwards. Often, they were teachers who we still admire and remember for their ways, their words and wisdom.

There were days when I learnt to love and sometimes hate, all in the same house, often on the very same day. There were times that taught me that justice and injustice were often inappropriate bed mates, that seeing things in black and white was never that simple in life.

Days when we were children in the morning and adults by bedtime, as innocence could be stolen so quickly without even knowing it. And for all we learned, we gained and for all we ignored, we lost. That education was priceless.

I now know how lucky I was to grow up in that environment at that time, as it served as my apprenticeship for a life in the Probation Service and in many other ways. Without those formative years, without those heroes and heroines, we are nothing, wherever we come from.

If you look back with honesty, trace your steps and recall your heartbeat, you may discover that amidst the ugliness and beauty of life that it was worthwhile, that you alone are worthwhile.

As Father Jim said, there's only one person responsible for doing their own dirty washing. And now I've looked back as honestly as I can, washing those dirty white shirts of my youth, I have rediscovered my good fortune in growing up on the Grove. If my only achievement has been to help my mother escape domestic violence, that will forever suffice in terms of finding my own freedom.

As for the estate of Red Bricks and Loose Dogs, there have been many changes over these past fifty years. People have passed by and passed away and even most of the buildings are now painted half white, maybe to bring some brightness and hope into that memorable environment. Maybe the world we knew has moved on forever. Maybe it hasn't moved on at all. But one thing is for certain, I will still carry it with me wherever I go and, no doubt, so will many others.

The End